Quiet-Time
DeVotioNS
for
Girls

JoAnne Simmons

Quiet-Time
DEVOTIONS
for
Girls

180 Days of
Comforting Inspiration

BARBOUR kidz

A Division of Barbour Publishing

Our mission is to inspire the world with the life-changing message of the Bible.

Introduction

The world out there is too *loud* sometimes, isn't it? Maybe you find yourself just wanting to put your hands over your ears or to put your earbuds in tight and tune everything out except what you want to focus on. Life can be loud from every direction too. So many people and things want you to pay attention *right now*. Your parents and loved ones and teachers and coaches, of course. And your friends and TV and phone and laptop and social media and chores and pets and homework all want you to pay attention too. Whew! It can be totally overwhelming! So you've got to take time to be quiet. And not just any kind of quiet will do. You need quiet time with the one true God who loves you like crazy and created you on purpose. The more quiet time you spend with Him, the more you learn about Him, the more you find out His good plans for your life, and the more you are filled with His love and wisdom and comfort and peace.

Why Should I Have
Quiet Time? Part 1

[People] become right with God by putting their trust in
Jesus Christ. God will accept [people] if they come this way.
All [people] are the same to God. For all [people] have
sinned and have missed the shining-greatness of God.
Anyone can be made right with God by the free gift of
His loving-favor. It is Jesus Christ Who bought them with His
blood and made them free from their sins. God gave Jesus
Christ to the world. [People's] sins can be forgiven through
the blood of Christ when they put their trust in Him.
ROMANS 3:22–25

The first and most important part of this book is to make sure
you know why spending quiet time with God even matters. It's
because how you relate to God is the most important thing
about you. Whether or not you have a relationship with God
affects every area of your life in the here and now, as well as
your eternal life. So. . .do you have a relationship with God?

Dear Lord, I want to be totally sure of
my relationship with You. Amen.

Why Should I Have
Quiet Time? Part 2

*God so loved the world that He gave His only
Son. Whoever puts his trust in God's Son will not
be lost but will have life that lasts forever.*

JOHN 3:16

This is what you need to know about relationship with God:
He created everything, including the first people, Adam and
Eve. But when they chose to disobey God, that sin spread
everywhere and put all the hard and sad things into the
world. But God made a way to beat sin and provide life
that lasts forever through relationship with Him. The Way is
Jesus! God showed the awesome love He has for all people
by giving His only Son, Jesus Christ, to die to pay the price
of sin for every single person who truly trusts in Him. And
then Jesus rose from the dead, proving God's power over
death—power that He gives to us when we accept Jesus as
the only Savior from our sin.

*Lord God, I'm so thankful You sent Jesus as the
Way, Truth, and Life (John 14:6)! Amen.*

Why Should I Have Quiet Time? Part 3

God has shown His love to us by sending His only Son into the world. God did this so we might have life through Christ. This is love! It is not that we loved God but that He loved us. For God sent His Son to pay for our sins with His own blood.

1 JOHN 4:9–10

The very best quiet-time prayer is something like this:

Dear God, I know I make bad choices sometimes, and I know I'm a sinner. Please forgive me. I trust that You sent Your Son, Jesus Christ, as the only Savior. I believe Jesus died on the cross to pay for my sin and that He rose again and gives me life that lasts forever. I want to give my life to You, Lord, and do my best to live like Jesus. I love You, and I need Your help in all things. Amen.

If you've prayed a prayer like that and meant it with all your heart, then you have a relationship with God and life that lasts forever, and nothing and no one can ever take those things away from you!

Dear Father God, thank You that I am saved because of Jesus, and I am Your child forever and ever and ever. Amen.

Built-In Best Friend

The truth is the Good News. When you heard the truth,
you put your trust in Christ. Then God marked you
by giving you His Holy Spirit as a promise. The Holy
Spirit was given to us as a promise that we will receive
everything God has for us. God's Spirit will be with us
until God finishes His work of making us complete.
EPHESIANS 1:13–14

Once you've asked Jesus to be your Savior, you suddenly
have a built-in best friend who will never leave you and will
always help you. That best friend is God's Holy Spirit. God
wants you to take quiet time and spend it focusing on His
Holy Spirit who is with you. You know you make good friends
with others by hanging out with them and getting to know
them more, and God wants you to hang out with Him too!
He sees all and knows all and loves you even more than all
the people on earth who love you best, and so He is the very
best friend to get to know and grow closer to.

Lord God, thank You for the Holy Spirit and
for being my best friend. I want to know You
better and better each day. Amen.

Superpower Love

Who can keep us away from the love of Christ?
Can trouble or problems? Can suffering wrong from
others or having no food? Can it be because of no clothes
or because of danger or war?...We have power over
all these things through Jesus Who loves us so much. For I
know that nothing can keep us from the love of God.
Death cannot! Life cannot! Angels cannot! Leaders cannot!
Any other power cannot! Hard things now or in the future
cannot! The world above or the world below cannot!
Any other living thing cannot keep us away from the love
of God which is ours through Christ Jesus our Lord.
ROMANS 8:35, 37–39

Sometimes we need quiet time with Jesus to rest from the
hard and sad things going on in our lives and in the world
around us. This scripture reminds us that not even one of
the very worst things of this world can keep us away from
God's superpower love for us through Jesus.

. . . .

Dear Jesus, You are almighty and so loving and good!
Thank You that absolutely nothing can stop your super
powerful love for me or keep me away from it. Amen.

The Greatest Is Love, Part 1

*If I know all things and if I have the gift of faith so I
can move mountains, but do not have love, I am
nothing. . . . And now we have these three: faith and
hope and love, but the greatest of these is love.*
1 CORINTHIANS 13:2, 13

You hear the word *love* everywhere these days, don't you?
Everyone talks about it, but what does it really mean? Why
do we love? Who should we love? Does it matter *how* we
love? If everyone has their own idea of love, is anyone right
or wrong about love? If there's no right or wrong kind of love,
then that would be confusing chaos! So it only makes sense
that there has to be one place where love came from first to
show us what true love means. And that first source of love
is God. 1 John 4:16 says that "God is love," and we can learn
about real, true love from His Word, the Bible.

*Lord God, I sure need Your help thinking about
all the different things the world tells me about
what love is. Please guide me with Your Word and
Your wisdom above everything else. Amen.*

The Greatest Is Love, Part 2

*Dear friends, let us love each other, because love
comes from God. Those who love are God's children
and they know God. Those who do not love do not
know God because God is love. God has shown His
love to us by sending His only Son into the world.*

1 JOHN 4:7–9

As you learn more about God and His love by spending quiet
time with Him, you'll be filled up so much you'll overflow! And
then you can give His love to everyone around you. It's the
best way to live: you come to God, receive encouragement
from His love, and share the overflow with others—then do
it again and again and again! You can continually repeat that
wonderful cycle of getting and giving God's love!

*Dear Father God, remind me every day who I am—
Your child. I know You, I know You are real love, and I
want to know You more. Please help me to show love
to others in ways that are just like Your great love.*

The Greatest Is Love, Part 3

Love does not give up. Love is kind. Love is not jealous. Love does not put itself up as being important. Love has no pride. Love does not do the wrong thing. Love never thinks of itself. Love does not get angry. Love does not remember the suffering that comes from being hurt by someone. Love is not happy with sin. Love is happy with the truth. Love takes everything that comes without giving up. Love believes all things. Love hopes for all things. Love keeps on in all things. Love never comes to an end.

1 CORINTHIANS 13:4–8

Spend some quiet time today reading and rereading these scripture verses. As you do, ask God to help you learn and understand more and more about His perfect true love. Ask Him to fill you up with it and help you share it generously with others.

Lord God, I believe You are love and what You say is love is what is truly love. Help me to keep learning and growing in Your real and perfect true love. Amen.

The Blessings of Family and Friends

A friend loves at all times.
A brother is born to share troubles.
PROVERBS 17:17

Who do you talk to the most or text the most? They are probably your closest loved ones and favorite friends! Spend some quiet time today thinking of all the reasons you love them and all the fun experiences you share. Think of all the times and ways you help each other with support and encouragement. Thank and praise God for putting them in your life, and ask Him to bless and guide them. If they don't trust in Jesus as their Savior, ask God to help you point them to Jesus as the one and only Way, Truth, and Life.

Dear Father God, thank You for the friends and family I have. Please help me to love and encourage them in the ways You want me to. Help our relationships to grow in all the best ways. Amen.

Each Morning

Let me hear of your unfailing love each morning,
for I am trusting you. Show me where to walk,
for I give myself to you. Rescue me from my enemies,
LORD; I run to you to hide me. Teach me to do your
will, for you are my God. May your gracious
Spirit lead me forward on a firm footing.
PSALM 143:8–10 NLT

Spending quiet time with God every morning is such a valuable thing to do. Like this psalm says, ask God to tell you about His unfailing love each new day. Ask Him to lead you and show you the good places to go and the good choices to make in your day—and to help stay away from the bad places to go and bad choices to make. Let the Lord teach you how to do His will.

Dear Lord, I want to begin my days hearing from
You. Please lead me and help me to do the good
things You have planned for me. Amen.

Each Night

*O God, You are my God. I will look for You with all
my heart and strength. . . . I have seen Your power
and Your shining-greatness. My lips will praise You
because Your loving-kindness is better than life. So I will
give honor to You as long as I live. I will lift up my hands in
Your name. . . . On my bed I remember You. I think of You
through the hours of the night. For You have been my
help. And I sing for joy in the shadow of Your wings.
My soul holds on to You. Your right hand holds me up.*
PSALM 63:1–4, 6–8

Don't just take quiet time with God in the mornings. This
scripture helps inspire you to take time each night too.
Actually, you can take quiet time with God any time of day!
The important thing is that you spend time praising Him
and praying to Him, listening to Him and learning from Him,
especially through reading the Bible, His Word.

*Dear Father God, remind me that any time of day
or night is a good time to spend with You. I'm so
glad You are always right here with me. Amen.*

God Faithfully Forgives

*If we tell [God] our sins, He is faithful and we
can depend on Him to forgive us of our sins.
He will make our lives clean from all sin.*

1 JOHN 1:9

When we know we've messed up and hurt a friend, sometimes we just want to stay away from her. We want to avoid
talking to her because we don't want to admit our mistakes.
We do that to God sometimes too. We avoid quiet time
with Him because we don't want to admit the ways we are
disobeying Him and making Him sad. But that's just silly. He's
so full of love and forgiveness for us. He wants us to simply
admit our bad choices and turn away from them and turn
back to Him instead. The good rules and guidelines He gives
us to obey are because He wants us to have the very best
kind of life and rewards both now and forever.

*Lord God, I admit my bad choices and my sins, and I
need Your help to turn away from them. Thank You
for Your love and grace and forgiveness. Amen.*

God Made You and Loves You

*You made the parts inside me. You put me together
inside my mother. . . . Your works are great and my
soul knows it very well. . . . Your eyes saw me before
I was put together. And all the days of my life were
written in Your book before any of them came to be.*

PSALM 139:13–14, 16

From the moment your life began and you started growing
in your mother's womb, God has been making perfect plans
for you. He created every detail of who you are; He knows
and loves you more than anyone else. And He made you with
free will—meaning you get to choose whether you will love
Him back and follow Him or not. You know forcing someone
to be your friend doesn't create a real relationship. And God
doesn't force anyone to love and obey Him either. He wants
you to love Him with real love that you choose. And when
you do, He wants to bless you with the very best kind of life,
the life He designed you for.

*Dear Father God, I'm thankful for Your real love
and for the free will You've given me. I want to
choose to love You back and obey You every day
of my life. When I make mistakes, please help me
quickly get back to closely following You. Amen.*

You Give God Joy

The Lord your God is with you, a Powerful One
Who wins the battle. He will have much joy over
you. With His love He will give you new life.
He will have joy over you with loud singing.

ZEPHANIAH 3:17

Doesn't it feel good to make someone happy and see them smile? In your quiet time today, think about making God happy and seeing Him smile. He does smile over you. You bring Him so much joy simply by being you. He loves you so much that He sent His only Son to die and pay the price for your sin so that He could have a relationship with you.

Almighty God, I'm amazed that even though
You are powerful over all of creation, You still
see little old me, and You love me and You smile
and experience joy because of me. Wow! I want
to grow closer and closer to You! Amen.

Worship Anytime and Anywhere

Call out with joy to the Lord, all the earth. Be glad as you serve the Lord. Come before Him with songs of joy. Know that the Lord is God. It is He Who made us, and not we ourselves. We are His people and the sheep of His field. Go into His gates giving thanks and into His holy place with praise. Give thanks to Him. Honor His name. For the Lord is good. His loving-kindness lasts forever. And He is faithful to all people and to all their children-to-come.

PSALM 100

With psalms like this and with your favorite songs you've learned about God, worship Him! Anytime, anywhere, even when you need to be quiet, you can focus on praising God in your mind and immediately be filled up with goodness and joy.

. . . .

Dear Father God, I want to praise You everywhere I go in everything I do! You are so good and so amazing! Amen.

Pray for Everyone

First of all, I ask you to pray much for all men and to give thanks for them. Pray for kings and all others who are in power over us so we might live quiet God-like lives in peace. It is good when you pray like this. It pleases God Who is the One Who saves. He wants all people to be saved from the punishment of sin. He wants them to come to know the truth. There is one God. There is one Man standing between God and men. That Man is Christ Jesus. He gave His life for all men so they could go free and not be held by the power of sin.

1 TIMOTHY 2:1–6

There are so many people in your life to pray for—everyone you know needs prayer! You don't have to know all their needs specifically, because God is so awesome that He already does. But He wants you to bring them before Him in prayer, showing that you care about them and want them to depend on God.

Dear Lord, I'm so thankful You care about every single person and You know every need. Most of all, I pray for more and more people to be saved from sin by choosing to believe in Jesus Christ as our one and only Savior from sin. Amen.

If You Respect Your Father and Mother

Children, as Christians, obey your parents. This is the right thing to do. Respect your father and mother. This is the first Law given that had a promise. The promise is this: If you respect your father and mother, you will live a long time and your life will be full of many good things.

EPHESIANS 6:1–3

Kids in your class, TV shows, social media. . .so many sources will give you the idea that it's not cool or popular to respect and obey your parents. These sources will tell you it's more fun to break the good rules you've been given, and even if you get in trouble, at least you'll be getting some attention for it. But what does God's Word say? It says to honor your father and mother, and this is the first command from God that comes with a promise. Sounds pretty important and worth it, doesn't it?

Dear Father God, even when I don't feel like it, or even when I feel pressure from the "cool" world around me not to, help me to do my very best to respect and obey and honor my parents. By doing so, I'll also be obeying You, and I trust You will bless me for it just as You've promised. Amen.

Your Good Shepherd

*The Lord is my Shepherd. I will have everything
I need. He lets me rest in fields of green grass. He leads
me beside the quiet waters. He makes me strong again.
He leads me in the way of living right with Himself which
brings honor to His name. Yes, even if I walk through
the valley of the shadow of death, I will not be afraid of
anything, because You are with me. You have a walking
stick with which to guide and one with which to help.
These comfort me. You are making a table of food ready
for me in front of those who hate me. You have poured
oil on my head. I have everything I need. For sure, You
will give me goodness and loving-kindness all the days of
my life. Then I will live with You in Your house forever.*

PSALM 23

Good shepherds take good care of their sheep, and the
Bible tells us how the Lord is our Shepherd, guiding and
protecting us through ups and downs. Spend some quiet
time today focusing on Psalm 23 and thanking and praising
God for His love and care.

*Dear Lord, I'd be so lost without You!
Thank You for being my Good Shepherd.*

24

His Sheep Hear His Voice

[Jesus said,] "My sheep hear My voice and I know them. They follow Me. I give them life that lasts forever. They will never be punished. No one is able to take them out of My hand. My Father Who gave them to Me is greater than all. No one is able to take them out of My Father's hand. My Father and I are one!"
JOHN 10:27–30

When you've accepted Jesus as your Savior, you've become a sheep! No, you won't grow fuzzy wool and start munching on grass, but you are *like* a sheep who follows a shepherd. You know you shouldn't do anything without being guided by Jesus. You love to hear His voice and obey it. And you can't hear His voice if you constantly listen to other things in this world. So quiet down every day and pray something like this. . .

Dear Jesus, I'm so grateful to be one of Your sheep. Help me to listen to Your voice more than I listen to anything else. I want to follow You always and enjoy life that lasts forever. Amen.

Matching Words and Actions

Let us not love with words or in talk only.
Let us love by what we do and in truth.

1 JOHN 3:18

Do some people you know say nice things but then do things that aren't so nice? We can all be guilty of that sometimes, and we need to be careful that we live honest lives—and that what we say matches what we do. When you spend quiet time with God, learning about Him through praying and reading the Bible and listening for His voice, remember that what God says *always* matches what He does. His words are *always* true, and He proved His great love for all people by sending Jesus to pay for sin. Romans 5:8 says, "God showed His love to us. While we were still sinners, Christ died for us."

Dear Jesus, I want to keep learning from
Your love and Your words and Your actions.
Please help my life to be a lot like Yours. I want to
love not just in words but in everything I do.

Love for the Very Best Book

How can a young [person] keep his [or her] way pure? By living by Your Word. I have looked for You with all my heart. Do not let me turn from Your Law. Your Word have I hid in my heart, that I may not sin against You. Great and honored are You, O Lord. Teach me Your Law. I have told with my lips of all the Laws of Your mouth. I have found as much joy in following Your Law as one finds in much riches. I will think about Your Law and have respect for Your ways. I will be glad in Your Law. I will not forget Your Word.

PSALM 119:9–16

The things of this world will distract us from the very best book—the Bible—but we are supposed to love it and long for it. That means we should crave it like our very favorite things! Every day we need to ask for God's help to be able to make this scripture from Psalm 119 true for us to say.

Dear Father God, I want to love and crave learning from Your Word. Help me to hide it in my heart and mind by reading it, listening to it, memorizing it, and living my life by it. Amen.

Every Good Gift

Whatever is good and perfect is a gift coming down to us from God our Father, who created all the lights in the heavens. He never changes.

JAMES 1:17 NLT

Take a big deep breath. Do you ever think about what a gift it is to do just that? The Bible tells us that every good gift is from our Father God in heaven and that "He is the One who gives life and breath and everything to everyone" (Acts 17:25). We can choose to focus on even the smallest of blessings we experience each day and to be full of thanks and praise to God. When we do, we'll be the happiest kind of people who love to share God's joy with others!

Lord God, I don't want to forget to thank You for even the blessings that seem the smallest in my life. Everything good comes from You. Help me to share this truth with others, plus all the joy that comes from being Your child.

Your Strength and Safe Place

I love You, O Lord, my strength. The Lord is my rock,
and my safe place, and the One Who takes me out of
trouble. My God is my rock, in Whom I am safe. He is
my safe-covering, my saving strength, and my strong
tower. I call to the Lord, Who has the right to be praised.

PSALM 18:1–3

In your quiet time today, focus on God as your strength, your rock, your safe place. If you're having trouble with home-work or friendships or stress at home, ask for His help. Let Him promise and reassure You that He knows what's going on and He cares about it all. He will help you with any kind of trouble when you depend on Him and follow His lead.

Dear Lord, thank You for being my strength and
rock and safe place. Please help me with my troubles.
You know what they are, and they are never too hard
for You to handle. I will trust and obey You in the midst
of them until You rescue me from them. Amen.

The Two Greatest Commandments

"Teacher, which one is the greatest of the Laws?"
Jesus said to him, "'You must love the Lord your God
with all your heart and with all your soul and with all
your mind.' This is the first and greatest of the Laws.
The second is like it, 'You must love your neighbor as you
love yourself.' All the Laws and the writings of the early
preachers depend on these two most important Laws."
MATTHEW 22:36–40

The most important things Jesus taught were these two things: First, love God with everything that is in you—all your heart, soul, and mind. And second, love your neighbor, meaning anyone around you, the same as you love yourself.

Sometimes you'll hear people say, "Jesus just says to love everyone. That's all you have to do." But they ignore the fact that He said before we love others we are to love God first and most of all. We can't love others in the best ways that God meant unless we first love God with all our heart, soul, and mind—and that includes getting to know Him through His Word and through prayer.

Dear Jesus, I want to follow Your
greatest commandments to love You
first and then love others. Amen.

The Lord Will Lead

*The Lord went before them, in a pillar of cloud during
the day to lead them on the way, and in a pillar of fire
during the night to give them light. So they could travel
day and night. The pillar of cloud during the day and the
pillar of fire during the night did not leave the people.*

EXODUS 13:21–22

Sometimes we wish God would lead us in perfectly clear ways
like pillars of cloud and pillars of fire in the sky, as He did with
His people, the Israelites, when they were wandering in the
wilderness. After all, sometimes we feel like we're wandering
in the wilderness too. We're not sure where to go or what
to do when we have problems and troubles in life. But God
knows how to guide us. He might not do it with such cool
ways as clouds and fire, but if we keep putting our faith in
Him and keep asking Him to help and keep listening and
watching for Him, He will lead us in exactly the ways we need.

*Dear Father God, I need Your help, and I'm
watching for You. Please guide me. Amen.*

Be Careful in Friendships

Do not let anyone fool you. Bad people can make those who want to live good become bad.
1 CORINTHIANS 15:33

Focus on praying for your friends in your quiet time today. We all need good friends in our lives, and we need to be good friends to others. But this verse makes it clear that we need to be careful in our friendships too. We need to know how to figure out if a friend is a good friend or a bad friend. Your very best friend is Jesus as your Savior. And the best kind of friends are those who love and follow Him too and try to be as much like Him as possible. A bad friend will want to lead you into trouble and away from following Jesus. We need God's help to know which friend is which! Never stop asking God to show you every friend's true character—and which friendships to keep and which ones to walk away from.

Lord God, thank You for the gift of good friends. Please guide me in friendship and help me to be careful who I'm friends with both now and in the future. Amen.

Chill Out

God has chosen you. You are holy and loved by Him.
Because of this, your new life should be full of loving-
pity. You should be kind to others and have no pride.
Be gentle and be willing to wait for others. Try to
understand other people. Forgive each other. If you have
something against someone, forgive him. That is the
way the Lord forgave you. And to all these things, you
must add love. Love holds everything and everybody
together and makes all these good things perfect.
COLOSSIANS 3:12–14

The last time you were mad at someone, did it help to
explode at them in anger? Or did it make things worse? When
people are driving you crazy, you definitely need quiet time
with God. Let Him chill out your anger and calm you down.
Let Him show You through His Word how He wants you to
act toward others—with lots of patience, grace, forgiveness,
and love, just like He's always giving to each one of us.

Dear Father God, please calm me down when
I'm upset with someone, and help me to treat
them with love like You do. Amen.

Baptized in the Name of the Father, Son, and Holy Spirit

Jesus came and said to them, "All power has been given to Me in heaven and on earth. Go and make followers of all the nations. Baptize them in the name of the Father and of the Son and of the Holy Spirit."

MATTHEW 28:18–19

If you have accepted Jesus as your Savior, have you chosen to be baptized? It's not something you absolutely *have* to do to be saved and go to heaven forever. The man who died next to Jesus when He died on the cross never had a chance to be baptized, and Jesus promised the man he would be with Him that day in paradise (Luke 23:42–43). But if you do have a chance, it is right to obey God's Word and follow Jesus' example. Baptism is a symbol using water to represent washing away your sin and choosing new life with Jesus. It's a way to show that you want to obey God and be like Jesus and that you are saved from sin and are His follower!

Dear Lord, please give me wisdom and courage about baptism. I want to obey You and show others how much I love You and want to follow You! Amen.

Wondering Why

We know that we belong to God, but the whole world
is under the power of the devil. We know God's Son
has come. He has given us the understanding to know
Him Who is the true God. We are joined together
with the true God through His Son, Jesus Christ.
He is the true God and the life that lasts forever.

1 JOHN 5:19–20

Do you ever wonder sometimes why bad things happen in
this world? Especially when you're in the middle of something bad happening to you? We all do. These things happen
because the whole world is under the power of the devil.
But those of us who believe in Jesus as our Savior belong to
God—so the devil can never, ever defeat us. The devil can
attack us and hurt us, but God gives us life that lasts forever,
no matter what!

Dear Father God, please give me extra love and wisdom
when bad things happen and I don't totally understand.
I trust that with Jesus as my Savior, no matter what
happens to me, I have life that lasts forever! Amen.

The One Who Forgives

If you, Lord, should write down our sins, O Lord, who could stand? But You are the One Who forgives, so You are honored with fear. I wait for the Lord. My soul waits and I hope in His Word. My soul waits for the Lord more than one who watches for the morning; yes, more than one who watches for the morning. O Israel, hope in the Lord! For there is loving-kindness with the Lord. With Him we are saved for sure. And He will save Israel from all their sins.

PSALM 130:3–8

Sometimes we might feel like we've messed up so badly, made such a big blunder or so many mistakes, that we can never be okay again. But God is the one who forgives. We can come to Him no matter how badly we've stumbled. We can admit our sin and let Him cover us with His mercy and grace.

Dear Lord, I'm so sorry. I can't believe I messed up this much. I admit what I did, and I need Your help. Thank You so much for being the one who forgives. I need Your grace and mercy so desperately. Amen.

Church Love

We have a great Religious Leader over the house
of God. And so let us come near to God with a true
heart full of faith. Our hearts must be made clean from
guilty feelings and our bodies washed with pure water.
Let us hold on to the hope we say we have and not be
changed. We can trust God that He will do what He
promised. Let us help each other to love others and to
do good. Let us not stay away from church meetings.
Some people are doing this all the time. Comfort each
other as you see the day of His return coming near.

HEBREWS 10:21–25

Do you love going to church? It's so important that you do. The Bible tells us that we need to meet together regularly with other Christians who love and trust Jesus as their Savior. We need to worship God and learn more about Him together, and we need to encourage each other and comfort each other and take good care of each other!

Lord God, thank You for all the other Christians
who are in my life and also for the ones all over the
world! Help us to love getting together at church
to grow closer to You and to each other. Amen.

Pray for Your Church

*Those who believed what Peter said were baptized
and added to the church that day—about 3,000 in all.
All the believers devoted themselves to the apostles'
teaching, and to fellowship, and to sharing in meals
(including the Lord's Supper), and to prayer.*

ACTS 2:41–42 NLT

The Church with a capital C is all believers everywhere, and
if you belong to a local church, you have a group of people
who are your church family. They all need your prayers. You
can pray for the protection of your church and the people
who come. You can pray for the pastor and leaders and
teachers and employees and volunteers of your church. You
can pray for the people who are members and the people
who attend. You can pray for your church to preach the good
news and follow God's Word and glorify Him in everything.
You can pray for God to bring more and more people to
hear His truth and experience His love at your church. You
can ask God to show you how you can be an active part of
your church.

*Dear Father God, I pray for my church, my church
family, and all those who need to come to my church to
learn more about You. I pray that You would help me
to serve and be active in my church all my life. Amen.*

Full of Joy and Peace

Be full of joy always because you belong to the Lord.
Again I say, be full of joy! . . . Do not worry. Learn to pray
about everything. Give thanks to God as you ask Him
for what you need. The peace of God is much greater
than the human mind can understand. This peace will
keep your hearts and minds through Christ Jesus.

PHILIPPIANS 4:4, 6–7

No matter what hard or sad things are going on in your day, your month, your year, and your life, you have reason to be full of joy, because you belong to God if you have asked Jesus to be your Savior. You have nothing to worry about and everything to pray about. And as you trust in God and pray to Him for your needs, with thanks for who He is and all He does, you will have peace and joy that no one can explain because they are so out-of-this-world amazing!

Dear Lord, I'm so very thankful that I belong to You
and that You take my worries and troubles and
replace them with incredible peace and joy!

Love Big and Forgive Big

*Most of all, have a true love for each
other. Love covers many sins.*

1 PETER 4:8

When you make a mistake, you don't want someone to remember it forever, do you? That's why it's so encouraging to know that our mistakes and sins can be covered up by love. Best of all, God's true love covers our sins when we accept Jesus as Savior and understand and believe that He showed the most important act of true love when He gave Himself up to die on the cross to pay the price for our sin. And when we try our hardest to love other people like Jesus does and to work on good relationships with our family members and friends, our love helps cover the mistakes we make in those relationships too. Because we love big, we can forgive big—just like Jesus does!

*Dear Jesus, thank You for covering my many
sins and mistakes with Your great big love.*

Care for Your Family

*Those who won't care for their relatives, especially those
in their own household, have denied the true faith.*

1 TIMOTHY 5:8 NLT

Family is so important, even if we don't always get along.
Of course we won't. The people we love the most are often
the ones we spend the most time with, and we're human
beings who make mistakes. So it's obvious that we will get
on each other's nerves and have fights and conflicts now
and then. But when we love big, we can forgive big. And we
can promise to give each other grace and always take good
care of each other like God tells us to in His Word.

*Lord God, I'm grateful for my family, and I love
them so much. Help me to remember that love and
thankfulness when I'm feeling upset or frustrated with
one of my family members. Help us to forgive each
other and have peace and joy and fun again. Amen.*

Children of God

*See what great love the Father has for us that He
would call us His children. And that is what we are.*

1 John 3:1

When we trust in Jesus Christ as our Savior, we then can
have a close relationship with God as our heavenly Father.
It's wonderful to have an earthly family but even better to
know we are in the family of the one true almighty God.
Sometimes conflicts or troubles in earthly families get so
big they can be sad or even scary, forcing someone to have
to stay away from certain family members. Maybe that has
happened in your family or you've heard about it in a friend's
family. That's why being part of God's family is especially
important, because we know that no matter what goes on
in earthly families, no matter how broken they might be, we
are always God's children and *no one* can break that bond.
And with the one true almighty God as our loving Father, we
have all His care and protection every single day of our lives.

*Dear Father God, I'm so thankful that above
all, You are my loving heavenly Dad who
takes good care of me now and forever.*

When You Get Punished

*There is no joy while we are being punished. It is hard
to take, but later we can see that good came from it.*
HEBREWS 12:11

What happened the last time you got in trouble with your
parents or at school? Did you instantly think of your punishment as something to be grateful for? Probably not. No one
usually does. But actually, if you think about what the Bible
says about punishment and discipline, you can choose to
see the good in it. The good grown-ups in your life are truly
helping you when they punish or discipline you in wise ways
for things you've done wrong. They're trying to teach you
things like safety and honesty and respect and responsibility.
In your quiet time today, ask God to help you appreciate
punishment and discipline, even if they feel awful at first.
Choose to learn from them, and let God show you how He
is maturing and teaching you through them.

*Lord God, please help me when I've done
something wrong and then have to face the
consequences. Even though I don't enjoy it,
I want to see the good in wise punishment and
discipline, both now and in the future. Amen.*

Your Times Are in God's Hands

But as for me, I trust in You, O Lord. I say,
"You are my God." My times are in Your hands.
PSALM 31:14–15

Do you enjoy thinking about what you want to do when you grow up? It's fun to dream of all the ideas and possibilities. There are so many cool jobs to do and places to live and people to get to know. But you might get overwhelmed thinking about all that too. How do you know which paths or jobs to choose? First, trust that you are God's masterpiece. He created you "in Christ Jesus, so [you] can do the good things he planned for [you] long ago" (Ephesians 2:10 NLT). And then remember that all your times, every moment of every day, are in God's hands. You don't have to figure out all your plans. You can dream and pray about them and trust God and let Him lead you day by day.

Lord, You are my God, and I'm so grateful my times are in Your hands. Thank You for creating me to do the good works You've planned for me to do. I'll keep trusting that You'll lead me, show me, and help me. Amen.

Because You Bear the Name of Christ

*Trials make you partners with Christ in his suffering,
so that you will have the wonderful joy of seeing his
glory when it is revealed to all the world. If you are
insulted because you bear the name of Christ, you will be
blessed, for the glorious Spirit of God rests upon you.*

1 PETER 4:13–14 NLT

You're going to get teased and insulted for being a Christian and doing your best to obey God's Word and His ways. Maybe you already have. What's popular in the world is often the opposite of what God's Word says is good and right. And when you don't go along with what's popular, there's a good chance you'll get made fun of. That's not easy, but you can handle it. You are strong and brave because God is in you! Keep on doing your best to obey Jesus. He promises to bless you, and His Holy Spirit never, ever leaves you.

*Dear Jesus, I'll follow You and be happy to be called
a Christian, no matter what anyone else says
about me. You make me strong and brave, and
You fill my life with blessings. Thank You! Amen.*

Be Willing to Wait

When God made a promise to Abraham, He made that
promise in His own name because no one was greater.
He said, "I will make you happy in so many ways.
For sure, I will give you many children." Abraham was
willing to wait and God gave to him what He had promised.
HEBREWS 6:13–15

Have you been praying for something, but nothing seems to happen? If God is saying, "Wait," it's hard to stay patient. So we need to look to examples of others who have waited on God and seen His promises come true. Like Abraham, we need to be willing to wait and let God work in His perfect timing.

Lord God, I struggle with being patient sometimes. I want
what I want right now, and I don't like to wait. But that's
selfish. Please help me with this. I need to keep trusting
in You and Your timing instead of my own. Amen.

Joy in the Lord

*I will give honor and thanks to the Lord, Who has
told me what to do. Yes, even at night my mind
teaches me. I have placed the Lord always in front
of me. Because He is at my right hand, I will not
be moved. And so my heart is glad. My soul is full
of joy. My body also will rest without fear. For You
will not give me over to the grave. And You will not
allow Your Holy One to return to dust. You will show
me the way of life. Being with You is to be full of joy.
In Your right hand there is happiness forever.*

PSALM 16:7–11

In your quiet time today, focus on the truth that God is
always with you! You can live with true happiness and joy
by keeping Him always in front of you—allowing Him to lead
you and obeying Him through all of life's ups and downs.

*Dear Lord, thank You for never leaving
me. Please stay up front as my guide.
I want to follow You and do Your will.*

Beauty from the Heart

*Your beauty should come from the inside. It should
come from the heart. This is the kind that lasts.*

1 PETER 3:4

Whether you think a lot about clothes and makeup or not,
everyone needs wisdom from God's Word when choosing
clothes and styles and looking in the mirror. Does real beauty
come from the outside? Definitely not. You might know
someone who always wears the coolest clothes and looks
super pretty but doesn't act very nice or treat others kindly.
Does that seem truly beautiful to you? It's definitely *not*. And
maybe you know someone who never has the latest fashions
and never follows the latest trends in hair and makeup, but
they have kindness and honesty and love just overflowing
out of them for others. Does that seem truly beautiful to
you? It sure is!

*Dear Father God, please help me always to have the right
idea in my mind about what true beauty is. People look
at the outside, but You look at the heart (1 Samuel 16:7),
and that's how I want to think of beauty too. Amen.*

48

Let Yourself Be Low

Let yourself be brought low before the Lord.
Then He will lift you up and help you.

JAMES 4:10

The New Living Translation says James 4:10 this way: "Humble yourselves before the Lord, and he will lift you up in honor." Being humble is the opposite of being proud and thinking too highly of yourself. It's good to be confident and have healthy self-esteem, but it's *not* good to brag and think that you're better than others or that you can never make a mistake or that you have no need for God in your life. Being humble means you know you mess up sometimes and need forgiveness and grace from God and others. And being humble means you know there are always ways you can learn and grow.

Lord God, please help me to understand the
difference between being proud and being
humble. Help me to be humble and ever aware
of how much I need Your grace and love!

Extra Quiet "Quiet Time"

The Holy Spirit helps us where we are weak.
We do not know how to pray or what we should
pray for, but the Holy Spirit prays to God for us with
sounds that cannot be put into words. God knows
the hearts of men. He knows what the Holy Spirit
is thinking. The Holy Spirit prays for those who
belong to Christ the way God wants Him to pray.
ROMANS 8:26–27

You might take quiet time with God and sit and think, *I don't know how to pray today.* That's extra quiet quiet time, and it's okay! Just tell God that. Talk to Him and remember that the Bible tells us that the Holy Spirit helps us when we are weak and prays for us. God knows our hearts and our troubles and what we need. He just wants us to come to Him for help and hope, even when we don't know what to say.

Dear Father God, I come to You today to spend time
with You even though I don't know what to say. But
I'm here, and I believe You love me and the Holy Spirit
is here to help me. You know my heart and thoughts
and everything I'm going through. Thank You! Amen.

Careful with Social Media, Part 1

So be careful how you live. Live as men who are
wise and not foolish. Make the best use of your
time. These are sinful days. Do not be foolish.
Understand what the Lord wants you to do.
EPHESIANS 5:15–17

Social media is such a big deal these days. It can be fun and
good in some ways, but it can be really bad for you too. It's
important not to get addicted to it. Do you have friends who
are already totally obsessed with it? Or maybe you're starting
to be obsessed with it yourself. If that's the case, you need
to let grown-ups help you set limits, and you need to train
yourself to set limits. Put the screens away and challenge
yourself to see how much fun you can have with zero social
media involved. And if you do have social media, be extra
careful about using it, always asking God to give you a ton
of help to use it wisely.

Lord God, I want to be wise and not foolish about social
media. Please help me with it and show me how to make
the best use of my time like Your Word tells me to. Amen.

Careful with Social Media, Part 2

Whatever you say or do, do it in the name of the Lord Jesus.
Give thanks to God the Father through the Lord Jesus.
COLOSSIANS 3:17

You might hear a lot about people being mean and bullying and arguing in nasty ways on social media—or watching and sharing things that are definitely not kid or family friendly, things that would make God sad. Even things that are horribly evil. If you ever do choose to be on social media, be sure to determine ahead of time to take absolutely no part in the bad stuff. Make a promise that you will use social media only in positive ways that encourage and help others. The world has enough mean and awful stuff going on; no one needs to spread around any extra!

Lord God, if I use social media, show me ways to use it for good, to encourage others and share Your truth and love. Please help me to stay far, far away from the awful and evil stuff on social media. Thank You! Amen.

Stand Strong under Peer Pressure

Do not want to be like those who do wrong. . . .
Trust in the Lord, and do good. So you will live in
the land and will be fed. Be happy in the Lord.
And He will give you the desires of your heart.
PSALM 37:1, 3–4

It seems like those who do wrong are everywhere. And sometimes it seems fun and harmless to be like them and just go along with whatever seems popular, even if you know deep down that what is popular is wrong. It takes strength and courage to stay away from those doing wrong, especially if you're feeling pressure from people you thought were your friends. But God promises that if you trust Him and do good, you will have everything you need, and He will give you the things that make you happy because first you are happy in Him!

Dear Father God, please help me to stand strong under
peer pressure. I don't want to be like those who do
wrong. I want to do what makes You happy. I trust
that's the best way for me to be happy too. Amen.

How Much Forgiveness?

Peter came to Jesus and said, "Lord, how many times may my brother sin against me and I forgive him, up to seven times?" Jesus said to him, "I tell you, not seven times but seventy times seven!"
MATTHEW 18:21–22

Sometimes the people you love the most are the ones who can drive you crazy the most. Can you relate? It makes sense. We spend a lot of time with the people we love most, and that means we have a lot of chances to bug and bother each other. But we also have more opportunities to love and forgive each other. The Bible says that because God loves and forgives us so much, we should do the same. We should forgive others as often as we need to—seventy times seven! That means however much you first think you might need to forgive, you need to go way above and beyond that amount—because God goes way above and beyond in loving and forgiving you.

Dear Lord, please help me do my best at forgiving others in over-the-top ways like You forgive me. Amen.

Don't Whine—Shine!

God is helping you obey Him. . . . Do all things without
arguing and talking about how you wish you did not have
to do them. In that way, you can prove yourselves to be
without blame. You are God's children and no one can talk
against you, even in a sin-loving and sin-sick world. You
are to shine as lights among the sinful people of this world.

PHILIPPIANS 2:13–15

How much whining and grumbling have you done lately?
That's not a very fun thing to think about, is it? But we all
do it, and we need to admit it and ask God to help us stop.
His Word encourages us to do all things with no whining,
complaining, or arguing. When we're positive and full of joy,
other people notice and are pointed to God's goodness and
love and salvation. So don't whine. Shine!

Lord God, please forgive me for the ways I whine
too much sometimes. I want to do better at shining
light for You by being positive and full of Your joy,
no matter what I'm doing or going through. Amen.

Asking God Hard Questions

*Will the Lord turn away forever? . . . Has His promise
come to an end for all time? Has God forgotten to
be loving and kind? . . . I will remember the things
the Lord has done. Yes, I will remember the powerful
works of long ago. I will think of all Your work, and
keep in mind all the great things You have done.*

PSALM 77:7–9, 11–12

If you're hurting and sad today, it's okay to take your quiet
time to ask God hard questions and tell Him all about your
sadness and pain, just like the writer of this psalm in the Bible
did. Sometimes in the midst of something hard, we wonder
where God is and if He's forgotten to take care of us. That's
when we need to focus hard on remembering all the good
things He has done for us in the past, in His perfect timing,
and trust that He will continue.

*Dear Father God, I'm sad and hurting right now, and
I have so many questions because I don't understand
You. But I choose to trust You, and I want to focus on
Your goodness in my life in the past and trust that You
will come through for me like You always have. Amen.*

God Created and Controls It All

"When you pass through the waters, I will be with you. . . . When you walk through the fire, you will not be burned. The fire will not destroy you. For I am the Lord your God, the Holy One of Israel, Who saves you."

ISAIAH 43:2–3

If you spend a lot of time learning about natural disasters, you could fill up with anxiety and fear. Things like volcanic eruptions, tidal waves, earthquakes, hurricanes, tornadoes, sinkholes, forest fires, and such are fascinating—but scary too. No human being can control them or stop them from happening. We can only study them, watch out for them, and make emergency plans for safety during them. Natural disasters should be a reminder to people that no matter how smart or powerful we think we are, we can never control the earth or weather. So we should always be reaching out for help from the one true God who *can* control it all because He created it all.

. . . .

***Lord God, You are an awesome Creator,
and I trust in Your love and care! Amen.***

Don't Hold On to Sin

Come and hear, all who fear God, and I will tell you what He has done for me. I cried to Him with my mouth and praised Him with my tongue. The Lord will not hear me if I hold on to sin in my heart. But it is sure that God has heard. He has listened to the voice of my prayer. Honor and thanks be to God! He has not turned away from my prayer or held His loving-kindness from me.

PSALM 66:16–20

When we pray, we want God to listen and answer, of course! To be sure that He will do so in His perfect timing, we need to admit to Him the wrong things we do. This is called confessing our sins. The Bible is clear that God forgives us and removes our sin as far as the east is from the west (Psalm 103:12), but we can't hold on to sin. We must admit our sins to Him.

Father God, I do make many mistakes, and I don't want to hide them or pretend like I don't. I confess these sins right now: _____. Please forgive me for each one. Thank You that You do! Amen.

Unchanging God

"I, the Lord, do not change."
MALACHI 3:6

Life involves so many changes from year to year and even from day to day. Big changes and little changes. Changes with friends and in your family. Changes at home and at school. Think about how you get new teachers and leaders at school and church as you get older. Think about how you grow out of toys and activities you used to love when you were younger. Change can feel strange or sad or overwhelming at times, so God's promise that He never changes is a wonderful one to hold on to. He is our one trustworthy constant no matter what new things are going on in our lives. Hebrews 13:8 says, "Jesus Christ is the same yesterday and today and forever." Amazing!

Dear Lord, thank You for being a constant comfort and help to me! You are my steady, unchanging strength, and I love You! Amen.

Trust the Lord with All Your Heart

Trust in the LORD with all your heart; do not depend on your own understanding. Seek his will in all you do, and he will show you which path to take. Don't be impressed with your own wisdom. Instead, fear the LORD and turn away from evil.
PROVERBS 3:5–7 NLT

Start now while you're young and don't even try to depend on your own understanding. Does that mean you get a pass on schoolwork? Ha! No, it doesn't. You should still learn about the world and the people around you, but as you do, you should trust that the Lord's ways are always higher than our human ways. We can't fully understand Him because He is just so above-and-beyond-us awesome! So trust Him with all your heart and seek Him in all you do. Then He'll lead you into an abundant life—a life full of the good things He planned for you to do when He created you.

Lord, I want what You want for my life. I trust You completely. Please help me to keep holding on tight to my faith as I follow You. Amen.

God Gives Good Things to Those Who Ask

*"You parents—if your children ask for a loaf of
bread, do you give them a stone instead? Or if they
ask for a fish, do you give them a snake? Of course not!
So if you sinful people know how to give good gifts to
your children, how much more will your heavenly
Father give good gifts to those who ask him."*

MATTHEW 7:9–11 NLT

God loves to bless you and give you good gifts, so pray big
and ask Him for the things you need and for the desires of
your heart. Never stop praying to Him and telling Him why
you need or want those things. As you draw closer to Him,
He will bless you—sometimes not in the ways you hoped
but always in ways you never dreamed of and that are best
for you.

*Dear Father God, thank You for wanting to give me
good things. I come to You and ask You for these
things: _____. I trust my life to You, and I trust You
to bless me in the ways You know are best. Amen.*

What Is Wisdom?

The fear of the Lord is the beginning of wisdom.
All who obey His Laws have good understanding.

PSALM 111:10

If you hear people talk about having wisdom, you might wonder what it is exactly. It's not just being smart and reading lots of books. It's not what you get once you're old and wrinkly. You can gain some kinds of wisdom by reading books and living a long time, for sure, but real wisdom comes only from the one true God. Wisdom is the ability to figure out right from wrong; it includes good sense and good judgment. Maybe that doesn't sound popular and cool, but God's wisdom really is awesome! Having it and using it makes for the best kind of life. And the Bible tells us that the fear of God (meaning faith in and respect for God) is the beginning of wisdom.

· ·

Lord God, I'm young, and I'm not sure I've ever
thought much about having wisdom. Could You please
inspire me to want to grow in this area and teach me
what You want me to know? Thank You! Amen.

Ask God for Wisdom

*If you do not have wisdom, ask God for it. He is always
ready to give it to you and will never say you are
wrong for asking. You must have faith as you ask
Him. You must not doubt. Anyone who doubts is
like a wave which is pushed around by the sea.*

JAMES 1:5–6

God loves you and cares about every single thing about you.
In everything you do and think and say throughout your
days—at home with your family, at school with classmates
and teachers, in your activities with friends, and even when
you're just hanging out by yourself—God wants to help you.
He wants you to ask for and use His wisdom as you make
choices and learn and grow. And don't doubt His wisdom.
He doesn't want you to be like a wave that's pushed around
by the sea. He wants you to use His wisdom to be strong and
stable, ready and able to do the good things He planned for
you when He created you.

***Dear Father God, please give me Your wisdom for
everything in my life. Help me to trust You and use
that wisdom exactly the way You want me to. Amen.***

No Sinful Thing

I will set no sinful thing in front of my eyes. I hate the work of those who are not faithful. It will not get hold of me. A sinful heart will be far from me. I will have nothing to do with sin.

PSALM 101:3–4

The writer of this psalm makes a big promise in this passage—the promise to look at no sinful thing. It was easier in his time to make that promise because there were no movies or TV shows or smartphones or TikTok or YouTube videos back then. And now there are. So we have to be extra careful of what we look at these days, because the world is so full of sinful things to look at—and our enemy the devil wants to push those things on us so that we'll disobey God and walk away from Him.

Dear Lord, I want to make this promise too—I don't want to look at or watch anything that is sinful. I want to keep my mind and heart clean and far away from sin. Please help me. Amen.

Always There, Everywhere

*Where can I go from Your Spirit? Or where can I
run away from where You are? If I go up to heaven,
You are there! If I make my bed in the place of the dead,
You are there! If I take the wings of the morning or live
in the farthest part of the sea, even there Your hand
will lead me and Your right hand will hold me.*

PSALM 139:7–10

There is no place on earth where you are ever away from God. Through His Spirit, He is with you every single second of every single day, no matter where you go and what you do. He sees and knows everything, even everything you think! That truth should never bother you; it should make you feel loved and cared for. God wants to help and guide and protect you anytime and anywhere.

*Dear Father God, thank You for being my
constant companion. You are always here,
everywhere! I'm never alone and have nothing
to fear when I depend on You! Amen.*

God Takes Sin Far, Far Away

*The Lord is full of loving-pity and kindness. He is
slow to anger and has much loving-kindness. . . .
He has taken our sins from us as far as the east is from
the west. The Lord has loving-pity on those
who fear Him, as a father has loving-pity on his
children. For He knows what we are made of.
He remembers that we are dust. The days of man
are like grass. He grows like a flower of the field.
When the wind blows over it, it is gone. Its place will
remember it no more. But the loving-kindness of the
Lord is forever and forever on those who fear Him.*
PSALM 103:8, 12–17

In your quiet time today, focus on thanking God for taking
away your sins. No one but God can do that, and He does it
in the best and biggest way. He takes your sins away from you
as far as possible—as far as the east is from the west. Amazing!

. . . .

***Lord God, I can never thank You enough for taking away
my sins because I trust in Jesus as my Savior. I want to
love and respect and obey You all my days! Amen.***

The Goodness of God's Word, Part 1

All the Holy Writings are God-given and are made alive by Him. Man is helped when he is taught God's Word. It shows what is wrong. It changes the way of a man's life. It shows him how to be right with God. It gives the man who belongs to God everything he needs to work well for Him.

2 TIMOTHY 3:16–17

God can communicate with us in any way He chooses. He shows us He is real by His amazing creation all around us. He proves Himself to us when we talk to Him and He answers our prayers. He shows us His love in endless ways and through so many people who take care of us and encourage us and bless us. And He speaks to us through the written word, especially through the Bible. We must choose to believe that the Bible is God's main way of teaching and guiding us, and then we must read it, follow it, and put its truths into action in our lives.

Dear Father God, please help me to love Your Word and the way You guide me through it. Inspire me to want to read it every day and learn more about You and how You want to guide me in the best paths for my life. Amen.

The Goodness of God's Word, Part 2

*God's Word is living and powerful. It is sharper than
a sword that cuts both ways. It cuts straight into
where the soul and spirit meet and it divides them.
It cuts into the joints and bones. It tells what the heart
is thinking about and what it wants to do. No one can
hide from God. His eyes see everything we do. We must
give an answer to God for what we have done.*

HEBREWS 4:12–13

God's Word is not just some ancient book that should look
nice sitting on a shelf. It is alive and powerful as we read it,
and God uses it to speak to us. After all, "everything that was
written in the Holy Writings long ago was written to teach us.
By not giving up, God's Word gives us strength and hope"
(Romans 15:4).

*Dear Lord, please speak directly to me through
Your Word each day. Teach me and help me to
listen and learn and obey You well. Amen.*

The Goodness of God's Word, Part 3

The grass dries up. The flower loses its color.
But the Word of our God stands forever.

ISAIAH 40:8

Since the Bible is the main source of wisdom God has given us, we should make it a regular part of our daily lives. We shouldn't just flip through it once in a while. We shouldn't just carry it to church and not touch it the rest of the week. If we spend time reading it regularly and praying to God as we do, we will learn more and more about God and His people and how He wants His Word to help us in everything we do.

- -

Lord God, please help me to love Your Word and
spend time reading and studying it regularly.
Help me to understand it. I want to hear from You
and grow in wisdom and draw closer to You! Amen.

What's Your Identity?

*And God made man in His own likeness. In the likeness
of God He made him. He made both male and female.*

GENESIS 1:27

Many people talk about trying to figure out their identity these
days. If we look to God, that's where we find it! His Word is
clear in Genesis 1 that God made us in His likeness. He has
created boys and girls to grow up into men and women, and
He has given us the Bible to guide us in how to live and love
like He does. Galatians 2:20 says, "Christ lives in me. The life
I now live in this body, I live by putting my trust in the Son of
God. He was the One Who loved me and gave Himself for
me." And 1 Peter 2:9 says, "But you are a chosen group of
people. . . . You belong to God. He has done this for you so
you can tell others how God has called you out of darkness
into His great light."

**Dear Father God, remind me every day that my
identity is found in You. Thank You for creating me
and saving me from sin! I live my life with trust in
You, following Jesus Christ, who lives in me. Amen.**

Give Your Way over to the Lord

*Trust in the Lord, and do good. So you will live in the land
and will be fed. Be happy in the Lord. And He will give you
the desires of your heart. Give your way over to the Lord.
Trust in Him also. And He will do it. He will make your being
right and good show as the light, and your wise actions as
the noon day. Rest in the Lord and be willing to wait for Him.*

PSALM 37:3–7

Today and every day in your quiet time, ask God to help you
rest in Him. Let your joy come from trusting in Him and doing
the good things He wants you to do. He gave you your life,
and you can let Him lead it. He wants to bless you in the best
kinds of ways both now and forever.

*Dear Lord, I don't want to be like those
who do wrong. I want all my happiness
and joy to come from following You,
resting in You, and waiting on You! Amen.*

Tell the Truth, Part 1

Stop lying to each other. Tell the truth to your neighbor.
EPHESIANS 4:25

Telling the truth is a big deal. Honesty is a key part of being a good person and having good character. The Bible says in Proverbs 12:22, "The Lord hates lying lips, but those who speak the truth are His joy." Since God hates lying lips, then so should we! And that means we should tell the truth about everything—big things and little things. Luke 16:10–12 says, "He that is faithful with little things is faithful with big things also. He that is not honest with little things is not honest with big things. If you have not been faithful with riches of this world, who will trust you with true riches? If you have not been faithful in that which belongs to another person, who will give you things to have as your own?" When we tell the truth, people can trust us, and God will bless us. He will be full of joy because of us!

**Dear Lord, please help me never to lie,
even about little things. I want to tell the truth
and be trustworthy in all things. Amen.**

Tell the Truth, Part 2

*Show me Your ways, O Lord. Teach me Your
paths. Lead me in Your truth and teach me.
For You are the God Who saves me.*

PSALM 25:4–5

Honesty and truth are super important, especially in a world
where they often seem harder and harder to find. Let God
and the Bible be your number one source of truth, and let the
following scriptures help you focus on how important it is!

- "The honor of good people will lead them, but
  those who hurt others will be destroyed by their
  own false ways" (Proverbs 11:3).

- "A man who tells lies about someone will be punished. He who tells lies will be lost" (Proverbs 19:9).

- "Do your best to know that God is pleased with
  you. Be as a workman who has nothing to be
  ashamed of. Teach the words of truth in the right
  way. Do not listen to foolish talk about things that
  mean nothing. It only leads people farther away
  from God" (2 Timothy 2:15–16).

*Lord God, You and Your Word are the ultimate
truth! Help me to love You and the Bible more
and more with all my heart. Amen.*

Don't Be Afraid of Them

"Don't be afraid of those who threaten you. For the time is coming when everything that is covered will be revealed, and all that is secret will be made known to all."
MATTHEW 10:26 NLT

If you've ever dealt with bullies in your life, you know they usually have to try to be sneaky to be mean. This scripture reminds you not to be afraid of them, because they will be found out—if not right away, then eventually. Teachers and school staff and other leaders in your life are usually on the lookout for bullies, so they will get in trouble. Above all, God sees and cares and will bring consequences and justice. Keep praying to Him to do that and to give you wisdom for standing up to bullies—and protection and courage too!

Dear Father God, remind me every day that I don't need to be afraid of anyone. You see and know all, and You will make everything right in Your perfect timing. Amen.

Let God's Word Live in You

Let the teaching of Christ and His words keep on living in you. These make your lives rich and full of wisdom.

COLOSSIANS 3:16

Everything that we put into our minds through our eyes and ears affects what we say and do. So this scripture in Colossians 3 helps us. If we let all the teachings of Jesus live in us—meaning we focus on, listen to, and obey them most of all—we will have lives that are rich and full of wisdom. (The word *rich* in this case doesn't necessarily mean a life of material wealth; instead it means a life full of all the goodness God wants to give us, especially the things money can never buy.) So as you make choices about what you put into your mind, you can ask yourself, *Does this help me to honor God and follow Jesus or not? If not, what could I choose instead that would help me focus on Him?*

Lord God, please help me to make even the smallest choices in my life with wisdom from You. Help me to say and do all things in ways that honor You! Amen.

Let Your Light Shine!

"You are the light of the world. You cannot hide a city that is on a mountain. Men do not light a lamp and put it under a basket. They put it on a table so it gives light to all in the house. Let your light shine in front of men. Then they will see the good things you do and will honor your Father Who is in heaven."

MATTHEW 5:14–16

Get up and tell yourself each morning as you look in the mirror, "You are the light of the world." That's what Jesus has said of us when we trust Him as Savior. With the Holy Spirit in us, we have an important job to do: we're to shine our lights so that others will want to trust Jesus as Savior and praise God too! We don't ever want to cover up our light. The dark world around us needs the good news and love of Jesus so very much, so let's do good things and be brave to shine as brightly as we can!

Dear Jesus, thank You for calling me the light of the world. I want to shine Your love brightly to everyone around me and give God all the praise! Amen.

The Way You Give

[Jesus said,] "Give, and it will be given to you.
You will have more than enough. It can be pushed
down and shaken together and it will still run
over as it is given to you. The way you give to
others is the way you will receive in return."

LUKE 6:38

Jesus clearly taught that we are supposed to be generous and willing to share what we've been blessed with. If we're selfish and keep all our blessings for ourselves, we won't see how God loves to give more and more to those who love to give. Aren't you grateful for the givers in your life? Who are the most generous people you can think of? Who are the most selfish? Who do you want to be like? Most of all, do you want to obey what Jesus taught about giving? These are good questions for all of us to ask ourselves regularly.

Dear Jesus, help me not to be selfish.
Help me to love giving to others and sharing
with others like You taught. Amen.

Who Made the Stars?

"To whom will you compare Me, that I should be like him?" says the Holy One. Lift up your eyes and see. Who has made these stars? It is the One Who leads them out by number. He calls them all by name. Because of the greatness of His strength, and because He is strong in power, not one of them is missing.
ISAIAH 40:25–26

When you get a chance sometime, spend your quiet time looking out at the night sky. Think about this scripture as you do. When you focus on the vast expanse of the sky and realize that God is so much bigger that He actually has a name for each of the billions and trillions of stars, your mind will be blown! We can't help but be filled with awe! How incredible that the same great big God who made the heavens and knows the stars by name made us and knows our names and takes good care of us too!

Father God, I can't even wrap my mind around how big and awesome You are! Thank You so much that I can talk to You and depend on You for anything. Amen.

Give God Your Worries and Cares

Give all your cares to the Lord and He will give you strength.
He will never let those who are right with Him be shaken.

PSALM 55:22–23

Life feels shaky—scary and unsure—sometimes, but God promises that those who are right with Him will never be shaken. (You are right with Him when you've asked Jesus to take away your sin and be your Savior.) What are you worried about today? What are you not feeling strong and sure about? Let God take those things away from you and give you His peace and power instead. First Peter 5:7 says, "Give all your worries to Him because He cares for you." What a wonderful heavenly Father we have, who loves us so much that He literally doesn't want us to worry about a thing! We can trust Him to take care of it all.

Lord God, I don't know why I hold on to worries so often, when You've told me You want to take them away from me. Please help me to do better and better at giving all my worries to You. I want to trust You more and have more of Your perfect peace and power. Amen.

Your Enemies

"You have heard the law that says, 'Love your neighbor'
and hate your enemy. But I say, love your enemies!
Pray for those who persecute you! In that way, you will
be acting as true children of your Father in heaven."
MATTHEW 5:43–45 NLT

Focus on your enemies during your quiet time today. Wait,
what? Why should anyone do that? Because Jesus said we
should. We are to love our enemies and pray for them, even
though that is *so very hard to do!* Jesus will help us, though,
and when we do love and pray for our enemies, we are acting
like true children of God.

Jesus, Your command to love and pray for the
people who are mean and unfair to me is not easy
to obey! But I want to do my best at this with Your
help because I love You and want to obey You.
It's only with Your grace and power that I can pray
for and love and bless my enemies. I'm trusting You to
help me, and I pray for these people right now. . . .

God's Got You Covered

But let all who put their trust in You be glad. Let them
sing with joy forever. You make a covering for them,
that all who love Your name may be glad in You.
For You will make those happy who do what is right,
O Lord. You will cover them all around with Your favor.

PSALM 5:11–12

When you're worried and scared about the troubles and
problems and enemies in your life, remember that God
protects you and provides for you. His Word promises that
He makes a covering for you. You probably know what it's
like to be out in the middle of a terrible thunderstorm, and
once you get to a covered and safe place, you feel so much
better! God is your covering and safe place in every kind of
storm that life brings. Don't forget that. Run to Him and have
protection and peace.

Dear Lord, thank You for covering me with
Your love and blessing and protection and care.
I don't know what I'd do without You! Amen.

Be Proud of Him and Praise Him

*If anyone wants to be proud, he should be proud of what
the Lord has done. It is not what a man thinks and says of
himself that is important. It is what God thinks of him.*

2 CORINTHIANS 10:17–18

When we reach a goal or accomplish something we've been working hard at, of course we feel happy and excited. It's time to celebrate! We just can't forget to give God credit for every cool thing we do. That's a great way to stay humble and never become full of pride in ourselves rather than in God. He is the one who deserves all the praise and worship because He is the one who created us and gives us all our gifts and abilities.

*Dear Father God, I want to be way more proud
of You than of anything cool I do. You are the one
who gives me everything. Please help me to use my
gifts well in the ways You want me to, especially to
share Your love and truth with others. Amen.*

Life Again for All Who Belong to Jesus

We want you to know for sure about those who have died. You have no reason to have sorrow as those who have no hope. We believe that Jesus died and then came to life again. Because we believe this, we know that God will bring to life again all those who belong to Jesus.

1 Thessalonians 4:13–14

When someone we love dies, we experience a sadness and pain that can never be fully fixed here on earth. We will miss them so much, and it's so hard not to be able to share our lives with them or hug them or even keep in touch by texting. But for all who believe in Jesus as Savior, this life on earth is not all there is. We have new life and perfect heaven to look forward to, where we will spend forever with Jesus plus all of our loves ones who believed in Him too. If you have loved ones who don't yet believe in Jesus, keep praying for them and asking God how to show them His truth and love.

Thank You, Jesus, for the peace and hope of knowing that I will be reunited with my loved ones who have died but who trusted You as Savior. Amen.

Work for the Lord

Work for them as you would for the Lord because you honor God. Whatever work you do, do it with all your heart. Do it for the Lord and not for men. Remember that you will get your reward from the Lord. He will give you what you should receive. You are working for the Lord Christ.
COLOSSIANS 3:22–24

In your chores and in your schoolwork, you might get tired or bored sometimes. Or you might think it all seems too hard. Take those feelings to God. Tell Him how frustrated or overwhelmed you are. He cares about your feelings. He will help you. You can do any task or assignment as if it's praise to God. Do your best at it, no matter what it is, saying to God, "Even though this work is hard or boring, I want to bring glory and honor to You through the way I do my best and have a good attitude in the middle of it." With that kind of approach to all your work, just watch how God will bless you in His perfect timing.

Dear Lord, remind me that no matter what I'm working on, I can do it in a way to bring You glory if I focus my mind on praising and thanking You in the middle of it. Amen.

Joy in Every Day

This is the day that the Lord has made.
Let us be full of joy and be glad in it.
PSALM 118:24

Maybe you've heard of the book and the movie *Alexander and the Terrible, Horrible, No Good, Very Bad Day* about a boy who feels like every single thing is going wrong in his day. We all can relate. And it's true that some days seem to have absolutely nothing good in them. Big things and little things go wrong, and we feel discouraged and defeated. But while our circumstances may feel awful, God's Word doesn't change based on our feelings. And His Word says, "This is the day that the Lord has made. Let us be full of joy and be glad in it." We can find reasons for joy in the midst of any bad thing—and the best reason for joy is that nothing can separate us from God's love or take away our perfect forever life that He gives us when we trust in Jesus Christ alone as our Savior.

Dear Lord, I want to be full of joy in each new day, no matter what is going on. Real joy comes from knowing and trusting in You! Amen.

Build on Solid Rock

[Jesus said,] "I will show you what it's like when someone comes to me, listens to my teaching, and then follows it. It is like a person building a house who digs deep and lays the foundation on solid rock. When the floodwaters rise and break against that house, it stands firm because it is well built. But anyone who hears and doesn't obey is like a person who builds a house right on the ground, without a foundation. When the floods sweep down against that house, it will collapse into a heap of ruins."
LUKE 6:47–49 NLT

We can read the Bible all day long, but it won't matter one bit if we don't actually learn from it and do what it says. Jesus taught that a person who listens to Him but doesn't obey Him is like a person who builds a house without a solid foundation. When floods come, the house will be destroyed. And when troubles come to people who only hear but don't obey Jesus, they won't be able to stand strong either.

Dear Jesus, You are my solid Rock. I don't just want to hear You; I want to obey You and stand strong on You, now and forever. Amen.

Close to God

Come close to God and He will come close to you.

JAMES 4:8

Since the Bible says God already knows everything you're going to say before you even say it (Psalm 139:4; Matthew 6:8), you might wonder why it even matters whether you spend quiet time with God and pray to Him. But maybe you have a close family member or best friend who can almost seem to read your mind that way too. If she knows you so well, then why do you care about spending time with her? Because you love her and have so much fun just being together and doing things together, right? That's the way God wants to be your absolute best, *best* friend. He loves you and knows you better than anyone else ever could, and He hopes you will want to simply spend time with Him and be included in the good things He is doing.

Dear Father God, I choose quiet time with You because I love You. I look forward to spending time with You as my very best friend of all. Amen.

Know Him Better and Better

I pray that the great God and Father of our Lord Jesus Christ may give you the wisdom of His Spirit. Then you will be able to understand the secrets about Him as you know Him better. . . . I pray that you will know about the hope given by God's call. I pray that you will see how great the things are that He has promised to those who belong to Him. I pray that you will know how great His power is for those who have put their trust in Him.

EPHESIANS 1:17–20

In your quiet time today, focus on how God wants these things for you:

- For you to have the wisdom of His Spirit.

- For you to know Him more and more.

- For you to have great hope in Him.

- For you to see what awesome blessings He has promised to all who belong to Him.

- For you to know how much power He has for all who trust in Him—the same great power that raised Jesus from death to life!

Almighty God, please help me grow closer to You, always learning more about Your promises, Your wisdom, Your hope, and Your power! Amen.

Above and Beyond

I pray that you will know the love of Christ. His love goes beyond anything we can understand. I pray that you will be filled with God Himself. God is able to do much more than we ask or think through His power working in us. May we see His shining-greatness in the church. May all people in all time honor Christ Jesus. Let it be so.

EPHESIANS 3:19–21

God's love is so above and beyond, so much bigger than anything we can ever even imagine, and He is able to do so much more than our greatest hopes and dreams! As you pray and ask for His blessings and help, think about the depth of His love for you and the goodness of His plans for your life—His ways are always the best! One day we will see exactly how He worked everything together for good for everyone who loves Him (Romans 8:28).

Dear Lord, thank You for Your great big love and awesome power! Thank You for working everything together for good in my life. I love You! Amen.

What to Do with a
Broken Heart, Part 1

*[Jesus said,] "I have told you these things so you may
have peace in Me. In the world you will have much
trouble. But take hope! I have power over the world!"*

JOHN 16:33

In this world, all kinds of sad things can happen to us or people
we know—loved ones and pets die, parents get divorced,
friends betray us. Houses burn down; favorite things get
stolen. People get sick or injured. Friends and loved ones
move far away, and we miss them. In any of those situations,
we have a very important choice to make—will we get closer
to God or drift away from Him? Will we choose to let Him
help and comfort us, or will we choose to hold on to anger
and blame toward God? The wise choice is to grow closer
to God. Psalm 34:17–18 says, "Those who are right with the
Lord cry, and He hears them. And He takes them from all their
troubles. The Lord is near to those who have a broken heart."

*Dear Father God, please help me choose to
draw closer to You when my heart feels broken.
Help me remember that You are near and You
want to heal my broken heart. Amen.*

What to Do with a
Broken Heart, Part 2

[God] heals those who have a broken
heart. He heals their sorrows.

PSALM 147:3

If you have a broken bone, you shouldn't run away, screaming angrily, from the doctors and nurses who can fix it. That would be dumb, right? You might want to run away because the process of mending the bone is painful and scary and feels like it will take forever. But much worse would be never fixing the broken bone at all. The same is true of a broken heart. God is the only one who can truly heal it. Choosing to get closer to Him when you have a broken heart doesn't mean you'll instantly feel all better. You will still hurt, and you might feel all kinds of emotions, including anger and fear. But if you let God, He will comfort you and help you with those emotions. It does take time to heal your broken heart, though, just like broken bones take time to heal. Keep praying to God. Keep reading the Bible. Keep going to church and letting other people who love God encourage you. God will show you His love and care in many different ways as He heals you.

Dear Lord, please help me remember that takes time
to heal my broken heart. Please comfort me. Amen.

Walk with the Wise

He who walks with wise men will be wise, but the
one who walks with fools will be destroyed.

PROVERBS 13:20

Think about the people you admire the most. What is it
about them that you admire so much? Is it their job? Is it their
talents? Is it how they treat you and other people? It's a great
idea to get in the habit now of asking smart and respectful
questions to grown-ups you admire. Ask them how they got
into the job or activities they are in. Or ask what it was like
to endure the hard things they've gone through in life. Be
willing and happy to have deep conversations with grown-
ups so that you can learn lessons from those who are older
and wiser than you.

Lord God, please show me wise people
in my life who I should learn from.
Thank You that I can look up to them. Amen.

Focus on Fruit

*The Holy Spirit produces this kind of fruit in our
lives: love, joy, peace, patience, kindness, goodness,
faithfulness, gentleness, and self-control.*
GALATIANS 5:22–23 NLT

Focus on fruit in your quiet time today. Not the kind in the
basket on the kitchen counter or in the drawer in the fridge.
Focus on the fruit from the Holy Spirit—the things that give you
good character and make you more and more like Jesus. God
wants you to be growing love, joy, peace, patience, kindness,
goodness, faithfulness, gentleness, and self-control in your
life. That's *a lot* of fruit to focus on and grow! But when we
ask God for help and truly want that kind of fruit growing
in our lives, He is happy to bless us with more and more!

*Dear Father God, I want to be more like Jesus and have
the fruit of the Spirit growing in me, filling me up like a
giant fruit bowl. I sure need Your help with this. Amen.*

Focus on Freedom

Be careful that you do not please your
old selves by sinning because you are free.
Live this free life by loving and helping others.
GALATIANS 5:13

Faith in Jesus Christ brings freedom—the very best kind. It's freedom from sin. Jesus paid the price for sin, and when we trust in Him as Savior, He removes it from us. That doesn't mean we'll never make bad choices again and suffer the consequences of them in this life, but Jesus takes away the forever punishment for those bad choices. And He helps us admit sins and want to get rid of them when we do make bad choices. Even though we have freedom from sin, we should never want to play around with sin. Instead, we should always want to use our freedom from sin to love and serve and help others.

Dear Jesus, thank You that I have the best kind of
freedom because You died on the cross to take the
punishment and pay the price for my sin. And then
You rose to life again—and You give me forever life
too! You are awesome, and I praise You! I want to
use my freedom to love and help others. Amen.

When Life Feels Heavy

[Jesus said,] "Come to Me, all of you who work and have heavy loads. I will give you rest. Follow My teachings and learn from Me. I am gentle and do not have pride. You will have rest for your souls. For My way of carrying a load is easy and My load is not heavy."

MATTHEW 11:28–30

What feels heavy in your life today? Maybe it's a big school project or drama among your friends. . . . Maybe you're fighting with someone in your family. . . . Jesus says to bring to Him whatever you have that feels heavy, and He will help you with it. He will give you a break from it and enable you to experience His peace and rest. Ask Him what to do about your heavy load, and then listen and let Him teach you, through prayer and through His Word.

Dear Jesus, please give me a break from my problems. I need Your rest and peace. Please guide me and show me how to deal with the hard things going on in my life in the way You want me to. Amen.

Be Bold and Speak Up

"Where is [Jesus]?" There was much talk among the people about Him. Some said, "He is a good Man." Others said, "No, He leads the people in the wrong way." No one spoke about Him in front of other people. They were afraid of the Jews.

JOHN 7:11–13

When Jesus was teaching on earth, some people who heard Him thought He was a good man, but they kept quiet because they were afraid. They didn't want to get in trouble with the Jewish leaders who were saying Jesus was a liar and a fake. As you grow up, ask God to help you never to be afraid of anyone who says Jesus is a fake. Those people might seem powerful in this world, but they are never more powerful than God. They are never more powerful than the good plans He has for you when you stay close to Him and stand strong in your faith. Be bold and speak up for Jesus, bravely telling others about Him, about the way He saved you, and about all the good things He is doing in your life.

Dear Jesus, I am proud of You, and I never want to be scared of anyone who says I shouldn't be! You are my Savior, and I love You! Amen.

No Shame

*I am not ashamed of the Good News. It is the power of
God. It is the way He saves men from the punishment
of their sins if they put their trust in Him. It is for the
Jew first and for all other people also. The Good News
tells us we are made right with God by faith in Him.
Then, by faith we live that new life through Him.*

ROMANS 1:16–17

Like the apostle Paul shared in Romans 1, we should all
want to be able to say this—that we are not embarrassed or
ashamed of the good news that Jesus came to earth to live
a perfect life and teach us, then died on the cross to pay
for our sins, and then rose to life again so that we can have
eternal life too, if we put our trust in Him. When we share
this good news with others, we help spread God's power to
save people from their sins.

**Dear Lord, please help me never to be embarrassed
or ashamed to share the good news about
Jesus! Thank You for loving all people and
wanting to save us all from sin! Amen.**

Be Happy with What You Have

A God-like life gives us much when we are happy
for what we have. We came into this world with nothing.
For sure, when we die, we will take nothing with us. If we
have food and clothing, let us be happy. But men who want
lots of money are tempted. They are trapped into doing
all kinds of foolish things and things which hurt them.
These things drag them into sin and will destroy them.
The love of money is the beginning of all kinds of sin.

1 Timothy 6:6–10

It's so easy to look around and compare what we have in our lives to what others have and what social media and TV say we should have. We need God's help to be content with the simple things in this life. If we have what we truly need, we should be grateful and happy, realizing that all other things are just extra blessings on top that we shouldn't always expect or feel entitled to.

Dear Father God, please help me to be happy with
having just what I need. Help me not to feel entitled
to more than that. Yet also open my eyes to the
ways You bless me with so many extras on top.
I'm so grateful for all Your goodness! Amen.

God Keeps His Word

God is not a man, that He should lie. He is not a son of man, that He should be sorry for what He has said. Has He said, and will He not do it? Has He spoken, and will He not keep His Word?

NUMBERS 23:19

Ugh, it stinks when people let you down. You know what that's like, right? No person can perfectly keep their promises, because we're all human, we all make mistakes, and things happen in life that we can't control. We should try our best to keep promises, for sure, but only God can keep promises perfectly. Sometimes people even straight out lie to us, and that's awful, but God never will. He keeps His Word, and we can trust Him.

Lord God, certain people have let me down in the past, so sometimes I wonder if You will let me down too. Please remind me that Your ways are far above and far better than the ways of people. You are the perfect promise keeper. You never lie or break Your promises. I can always hope and trust in You. Amen.

Let God Do the Fighting

Moses said to the people, "Do not be afraid! Be strong, and see how the Lord will save you today. For the Egyptians you have seen today, you will never see again. The Lord will fight for you. All you have to do is keep still."
EXODUS 14:13–14

If you read your Bible, you will see so many times when God worked in miraculous, against-all-odds ways to save and help His people. In your quiet time today, read more of the stories of Moses and the Israelites and ponder how God can help with any problem you have, no matter how big and horrible it seems. He will fight for you. Keep coming to Him for help and peace.

Lord God, You know exactly what I'm going through. You know the problems and enemies I face. You know my fears and worries. You know how to solve all the problems and defeat any bad guys. Help me to be still and strong as I pray to You. I'm depending on You! I believe You will do the fighting for me and come to my rescue. Amen.

Pray for All Protectors

*"No one can have greater love than
to give his life for his friends."*

JOHN 15:13

Do you have any family members or friends who serve in the military or on a police force? They are protectors of our safety and freedom, and we should be grateful for them and for all of the protectors in our nation and in our communities. Spend your quiet time today thanking God for them. You can think of ways to honor and encourage them too—things like taking treats to share with your local police station, sending cards and packages to service members who are overseas, and thanking a person in military uniform for their service. Most importantly, you can pray for their safety as they work to keep others safe and free. Especially pray that each one would know Jesus as their Savior!

. . . .

*Dear Father God, please bless and help our
protectors in the very best kind of ways.
Thank You for their bravery and sacrifices. Amen.*

Jesus Loves You

At that time the followers came to Jesus. They said,
"Who is the greatest in the holy nation of heaven?"
Jesus took a little child and put him among them.
He said, "For sure, I tell you, unless you have a change
of heart and become like a little child, you will not get
into the holy nation of heaven. Whoever is without
pride as this little child is the greatest in the holy nation
of heaven. Whoever receives a little child because of
Me receives Me. But whoever is the reason for one of
these little children who believe in Me to fall into sin,
it would be better for him to have a large rock put
around his neck and to be thrown into the sea."

MATTHEW 18:1–6

Jesus showed that He loves kids so very much, and that
includes you right now too! He even told adults to be more
like kids by being humble, meaning without pride, full of faith,
and totally dependent on our Father in heaven.

· ·

Dear Jesus, thank You for showing how much You
love kids like me. I want to love You back with my
whole heart. Help me always to be humble, trusting
and depending on my heavenly Father. Amen.

Don't Worry

*"I tell you this: Do not worry about your life.
Do not worry about what you are going to eat and
drink. Do not worry about what you are going to
wear. . . . Look at the birds in the sky. They do not
plant seeds. They do not gather grain. They do not
put grain into a building to keep. Yet your Father
in heaven feeds them! Are you not more important
than the birds? . . . Do not worry. Do not keep saying,
'What will we eat?' or, 'What will we drink?' or,
'What will we wear?' The people who do not know
God are looking for all these things. Your Father in
heaven knows you need all these things. First of all,
look for the holy nation of God. Be right with Him.
All these other things will be given to you also."*

MATTHEW 6:25–26, 31–33

"No worries," we often say, and we can really, truly mean it
when we trust in Jesus. In your quiet time today, focus on
His teaching about why we shouldn't worry.

. . . .

***Dear Jesus, please help me remember that You have
said I shouldn't worry about anything when I've
made the choice to trust You with my life. Amen.***

Look to What Can't Be Seen

Our spirits are getting stronger every day. The little troubles
we suffer now for a short time are making us ready for the
great things God is going to give us forever. We do not look
at the things that can be seen. We look at the things that
cannot be seen. The things that can be seen will come to an
end. But the things that cannot be seen will last forever.
2 CORINTHIANS 4:16–18

Especially when they pile up, the troubles of life can feel
so awful and overwhelming. Hard homework and endless chores and unwanted drama with friends. Or maybe
troubles that are far worse, like money problems in your
family or serious sickness affecting you or someone you
love. So we have to remember that the Bible says that every
trouble we go through now is getting us ready for the best
things God has for us forever. In heaven someday, we'll
go through no troubles at all. If we focus our thoughts on
all the wonderful things we can't see yet, which God has
promised, we'll get through the hard things that are part
of our lives right now.

Dear Lord, I'm excited for the good things You're
going to give forever to all who love and trust in
You. I want to focus on those things as You help
me get through earthly troubles today. Amen.

Your Tongue Is Powerful, Part 1

We make a horse go wherever we want it to go by a small bit in its mouth. We turn its whole body by this. Sailing ships are driven by strong winds. But a small rudder turns a large ship whatever way the man at the wheel wants the ship to go. The tongue is also a small part of the body, but it can speak big things. See how a very small fire can set many trees on fire. The tongue is a fire.

JAMES 3:3–6

The tongue is powerful, and our words matter a lot. So we must remember that God says we need to watch our words and be careful with them. Proverbs 21:23 says, "He who watches over his mouth and his tongue keeps his soul from troubles." And Ephesians 4:29 says, "Watch your talk! No bad words should be coming from your mouth. Say what is good. Your words should help others grow as Christians."

Father God, please help me to remember that the words I say matter and are powerful. Please help me to use my mouth and tongue wisely. Amen.

Your Tongue Is Powerful, Part 2

If a person thinks he is religious, but does not keep his tongue from speaking bad things, he is fooling himself. His religion is worth nothing.

JAMES 1:26

If we say we love and follow Jesus as our Savior, then we need to care about the words we say and the power of those words. And if we mess up and say bad things or lies, we need to confess and correct that sin as quickly as possible. Here are more scriptures that help us:

- "A gentle answer turns away anger, but a sharp word causes anger. The tongue of the wise uses much learning in a good way, but the mouth of fools speaks in a foolish way" (Proverbs 15:1–2).

- "The one who talks much will for sure sin, but he who is careful what he says is wise" (Proverbs 10:19).

- "If you want joy in your life and have happy days, keep your tongue from saying bad things and your lips from talking bad about others" (1 Peter 3:10).

Lord God, like Psalm 141:3 says, please "put a watch over my mouth. Keep watch over the door of my lips." Thank You! Amen.

The Lord's Timing

*Dear friends, remember this one thing, with the Lord one
day is as 1,000 years, and 1,000 years are as one day.
The Lord is not slow about keeping His promise as some
people think. He is waiting for you. The Lord does not
want any person to be punished forever. He wants all
people to be sorry for their sins and turn from them.*

2 PETER 3:8–9

God is so much bigger and more amazing than what our
brains can understand—including the way He views time.
This scripture shows us why we need to be patient when it
seems like God isn't keeping His promises. He is not being
slow or ignoring us. His main goal is to save as many people
as possible from their sins and give them eternal life in paradise, and He is accomplishing this goal through His perfect
plans. We can trust Him.

*Dear Lord, I'm sorry I struggle to wait on You
sometimes. Please keep reminding me how
much You love all people and how perfect
Your plans and timing always are. Amen.*

When There's Trouble

*Pray and give thanks for those who make trouble
for you. Yes, pray for them instead of talking against
them. Be happy with those who are happy. Be sad
with those who are sad. Live in peace with each other.
Do not act or think with pride. Be happy to be with
poor people. Keep yourself from thinking you
are so wise. When someone does something bad
to you, do not pay him back with something bad.
Try to do what all [people] know is right and good.
As much as you can, live in peace with all [people].*
ROMANS 12:14–18

If someone has been making trouble for you, make sure you
take extra quiet time with God. He will help you handle it in
the right way. Ask for His wisdom and strength, and let His
Word guide you.

. . . .

***Lord God, I need Your help dealing with this trouble
and the person who is causing it. I don't know
exactly what to do, but I trust You to show me.
Please give me wisdom and strength, and help me
work things out with love and peace. Amen.***

Joy Is Better Than Happiness, Part 1

Being with You is to be full of joy.
In Your right hand there is happiness forever.

PSALM 16:11

Whatever makes you happy! You might hear that saying a lot these days, but it's one to be careful with—because if our constant goal is just to be happy, we can truly ruin our lives. Think of it this way: Some people might be happy with junk food all the time, but it sure isn't good for them. And a lot of people would be happy to be on vacation every single day, but how would they earn money to live? Junk food and vacation can make us all really happy, but they have to be balanced wisely with healthy foods and times of work and learning. That's why joy is so much more important than happiness. Real joy is based on a relationship with Jesus and the hope of a perfect eternity with Him, while happiness is based on the circumstances we find ourselves in. When we focus on real joy and choose to be joyful in everything we do, then we can also find happiness in pretty much anything!

Dear Father God, deepen my understanding of how
real joy in You is far better than just happiness. Amen.

Joy Is Better Than Happiness, Part 2

"The joy of the Lord is your strength."

NEHEMIAH 8:10

Our feelings change so quickly and easily. Something that made you happy last year or even a month ago might seem totally boring or silly to you now. That's another example of how real joy is so much better than happiness. Focus on these scriptures in your quiet time today to learn more about real joy:

- "I have placed the Lord always in front of me. Because He is at my right hand, I will not be moved. And so my heart is glad. My soul is full of joy" (Psalm 16:8–9).

- "You have never seen Him but you love Him. You cannot see Him now but you are putting your trust in Him. And you have joy so great that words cannot tell about it. You will get what your faith is looking for, which is to be saved from the punishment of sin" (1 Peter 1:8–9).

Lord God, no matter what my emotions feel like, help me remember that true joy is always found in You.

Pray Like This

[Jesus said,] "Pray like this: Our Father in heaven,
may your name be kept holy. May your Kingdom come
soon. May your will be done on earth, as it is in heaven.
Give us today the food we need, and forgive us our sins,
as we have forgiven those who sin against us. And don't let
us yield to temptation, but rescue us from the evil one."

MATTHEW 6:9–13 NLT

In your quiet time today, focus on Jesus' example of how we should pray. Praise God for who He is and for His awesome holiness. Ask for His kingdom to come and His will to be done. Ask Him to meet your needs day by day. Ask for the forgiveness of your sins as you forgive those who sin against you. And ask for protection against sin and the evil one.

Dear Jesus, thank You for teaching us how
to pray. Help me to remember and learn
from Your perfect example. Amen.

Quiet Time in Creation

"But ask the wild animals, and they will teach you. Ask the birds of the heavens, and let them tell you. Or speak to the earth, and let it teach you. Let the fish of the sea make it known to you. Who among all these does not know that the hand of the Lord has done this? In His hand is the life of every living thing and the breath of all men."

JOB 12:7–10

Spending quiet time with God out in His wonderful creation is so beneficial! In your backyard or at a park, in the mountains or at the beach, in the woods or by a river—God's creation and His creatures give us so much reason to praise Him! He made every good thing, and His power and goodness are brilliantly clear when we focus on all He has made.

Dear Father God, I praise You for how awesome You are! Your creation is spectacular, and I'm grateful You bless us with so many beautiful places and creatures in this world. Amen.

God's Angels

Because you have made the Lord your safe place, and the Most High the place where you live, nothing will hurt you. No trouble will come near your tent. For He will tell His angels to care for you and keep you in all your ways. They will hold you up in their hands.
PSALM 91:9–12

A lot of stories get made up about angels, and many are totally fiction. But angels themselves are not fiction. The Bible says they are real, and they help take care of you and protect you! Isn't that awesome? Hebrews 1:14 says, "Are not all the angels spirits who work for God? They are sent out to help those who are to be saved from the punishment of sin." And you can look up many other verses in the Bible about angels too—and be stronger and braver knowing that God can send them to help you with anything at any time.

Lord God, thinking about angels and how You send them to help and rescue people is so encouraging! You are awesome, Lord, and I love You. I'm so thankful to be Your child! Amen.

Positive Thinking, Part 1

*Keep your minds thinking about whatever is true,
whatever is respected, whatever is right, whatever
is pure, whatever can be loved, and whatever is
well thought of. If there is anything good and worth
giving thanks for, think about these things.*

PHILIPPIANS 4:8

This scripture is tough to follow sometimes. On grumpy days and when things go wrong, our first thoughts aren't usually happy, thankful ones. But God wants us to try to get rid of bad thoughts and keep our minds thinking positively. When we focus on praise and gratitude to Him most of all (and on the many things that are right and true in our lives), we keep our thoughts in the best places. When negative and nasty thoughts try to take over our minds, we can think of popping them like a bubble to make them disappear. Then we should blow positive bubbles into our brains that are full of God's goodness and love.

*Father God, please help me to keep my brain
thinking about what is good for me—most of all
You, because You are so awesome! Amen.*

Positive Thinking, Part 2

Do not act like the sinful people of the world. Let God change your life. First of all, let Him give you a new mind. Then you will know what God wants you to do. And the things you do will be good and pleasing and perfect.

ROMANS 12:2

God wants to give you a new mind full of thoughts that are focused on Him—thoughts that are wise and right and true! Check out these verses too:

- "If your sinful old self is the boss over your mind, it leads to death. But if the Holy Spirit is the boss over your mind, it leads to life and peace" (Romans 8:6).

- "You will keep in perfect peace all who trust in you, all whose thoughts are fixed on you!" (Isaiah 26:3 NLT).

- "If then you have been raised with Christ, keep looking for the good things of heaven. This is where Christ is seated on the right side of God. Keep your minds thinking about things in heaven" (Colossians 3:1–2).

Dear Lord, please be the boss of my mind through Your Holy Spirit. Amen.

The Story of Saul

*All at once [Saul] saw a light from heaven shining
around him. He fell to the ground. Then he heard a
voice say, "Saul, Saul, why are you working so hard
against Me?" Saul answered, "Who are You, Lord?"
He said, "I am Jesus, the One Whom you are working
against. You hurt yourself by trying to hurt Me."
Saul was shaken and surprised. Then he said, "What do
You want me to do, Lord?" The Lord said to him, "Get
up! Go into the city and you will be told what to do."*
ACTS 9:3–6

If you read the whole story of Saul (also known as Paul) in
the Bible, you'll be amazed at how Jesus totally turned his
life around. Saul had hated Christians to the point of killing
them, and then God confronted him and worked a miracle
in his life so that he became one of the greatest followers
of Jesus. God can do this for anyone, so keep on praying for
those you know who need a miracle like Saul did.

*Dear Father God, I pray for these people
right now, _____, who need a miracle to
learn to love and follow You. Amen.*

If You Obey the Lord

"Be faithful in obeying the Lord your God. Be careful to keep all His Laws which I tell you today. And the Lord your God will set you high above all the nations of the earth. All these good things will come upon you if you will obey the Lord your God. Good will come to you in the city, and good will come to you in the country. Good will come to your children, and the fruit of your ground, and the young of your animals. Your cattle and flock will have many young ones. Good will come to your basket and your bread pan. Good will come to you when you come in, and when you go out."

DEUTERONOMY 28:1–6

God clearly says in His Word that if we His people obey Him, He will bless us in every area of our lives. And who can bless better than the one true God who created everything and is the giver of every good gift?

Lord God, I want to obey You because I love You, and I trust You will bless me and bring good to me in countless ways when I do. You have promised to bless Your people for their obedience, and You always keep Your promises. Thank You! Amen.

Get and Give Comfort

*[God] gives us comfort in all our troubles. Then we
can comfort other people who have the same troubles.
We give the same kind of comfort God gives us. As we
have suffered much for Christ and have shared in His
pain, we also share His great comfort. But if we are in
trouble, it is for your good. And it is so you will be saved
from the punishment of sin. If God comforts us, it is for
your good also. You too will be given strength not to give
up when you have the same kind of trouble we have.*

2 CORINTHIANS 1:4–6

When you feel confused about hard or sad things in your life
and in this world, focus on this scripture. God will comfort
you in the middle of painful times, and then you can comfort
others with His love and care too. And one day when Jesus
returns to make all things new, we'll never experience any
sadness or pain again.

*Father God, help me to feel Your comfort in the
hard times and then comfort and encourage
others who are going through the same kind of
hard things. Help me to point everyone I can to
You, encouraging them to be saved from their
sins through faith in Jesus Christ. Amen.*

Pray for Our Nation

Pray for kings and all others who are in power over us so we might live quiet God-like lives in peace. It is good when you pray like this. It pleases God Who is the One Who saves.

1 TIMOTHY 2:2–3

Pray for our nation in your quiet time today. Understanding what all is going on with government and leaders can be confusing and frustrating, and since you're a kid and can't vote, you might think there's nothing you can do. But there is always something—you can pray, of course! Pray for the leaders of our nation—the president and vice president and their families and all elected officials at all levels of government and their families too. Praying for so many people might seem overwhelming, but you can think of the American flag as a reminder. Every time you see it, pray something like this:

Lord God, please bless our nation according to Your will. Help our leaders want to honor You. Please give them Your wisdom to govern well. May each of them know You as the one true God and Savior. Please protect our nation and protect our freedom to worship You, and help us to use that freedom to spread Your truth and love. Amen.

Pray for the World

*"Be still, and know that I am God! I will be honored by
every nation. I will be honored throughout the world."*
PSALM 46:10 NLT

You can pray specifically for each state in our nation too.
You might want to put a map on a wall somewhere in your
house and let it remind you to pray. You could also make a
chart listing people you know in each state and remember
them in prayer too.

And don't stop there. God loves everyone everywhere in
the whole world, not just our nation. So get a globe and start
praying for every person in every country and for all nations
to honor the one true God and to do His will according to
His Word.

*Dear Lord, You love all people of all nations, and You
want them to honor You and trust Jesus as Savior so
You can give them eternal life. You are such a good
and loving heavenly Father. Help me to remember
to pray for all people everywhere! Amen.*

Chin Up, Eyes Up

*I will lift up my eyes to the mountains. Where will
my help come from? My help comes from the Lord,
Who made heaven and earth. He will not let your feet
go out from under you. He Who watches over you
will not sleep. . . . The sun will not hurt you during
the day and the moon will not hurt you during the
night. The Lord will keep you from all that is sinful.
He will watch over your soul. The Lord will watch
over your coming and going, now and forever.*

PSALM 121:1–3, 6–8

"Chin up" is a saying you might hear to motivate and encourage someone who is feeling down. And the best kind of "chin
up" is with eyes toward God in heaven. He is where all your
help comes from. And since He is the Creator of everything
who holds all the universe together, never sleeps, and always
watches over you, you can feel brave and strong to deal with
any hard or sad or scary thing that comes your way.

*Dear Father God, please help me to keep
my chin up and my eyes up, always looking
to You for help and hope. Amen.*

With Trust and Confidence

We have a great Religious Leader Who has made the way for man to go to God. He is Jesus, the Son of God, Who has gone to heaven to be with God. Let us keep our trust in Jesus Christ. Our Religious Leader understands how weak we are. Christ was tempted in every way we are tempted, but He did not sin. Let us go with complete trust to the throne of God. We will receive His loving-kindness and have His loving-favor to help us whenever we need it.

HEBREWS 4:14–16

It can be kind of scary and intimidating to talk with well-known people and important leaders, right? So how cool that God's Word tells us that Jesus made the way for us to go to God, who is the King of kings, with total trust and confidence! We can even call Him "Abba" (Romans 8:15 NLT), which is a term like "Daddy"—that's how close a relationship we can have with the one true Creator God who is Lord of all!

Dear Abba, I'm amazed by Your power and might as the King of all kings, and yet You love me so much that I can come with confidence to Your throne and even call You Daddy. Thank You! Amen.

Laughter and Joy

We were filled with laughter, and we sang for
joy. And the other nations said, "What amazing
things the LORD has done for them." Yes, the LORD
has done amazing things for us! What joy!
PSALM 126:2–3 NLT

Aren't you glad God made us able to laugh? It's so good for us to be merry and glad and joyful! Proverbs 17:22 says, "A glad heart is good medicine, but a broken spirit dries up the bones." Who are your favorite people to laugh with? Spend your quiet time today thanking God for their part in your life and the joy they bring you. Ask God to help you all grow closer to Him, the source of all true joy.

Lord God, I love to laugh and have fun, especially
with family and friends. Thank You for my favorite
people who share so much joy with me. Please help
us draw ever closer to You, because You are the
giver of all real joy that will last forever. Amen.

Store Stuff in Heaven, Not on Earth

*"Do not gather together for yourself riches of this
earth. They will be eaten by bugs and become rusted.
Men can break in and steal them. Gather together riches
in heaven where they will not be eaten by bugs or become
rusted. Men cannot break in and steal them. For wherever
your riches are, your heart will be there also."*

MATTHEW 6:19–21

Jesus taught us to be careful with "stuff" here on earth
because we should be storing up riches for ourselves in
heaven, not on earth. No matter how much we love what we
own, we can't take any of it to heaven with us when we die,
so we shouldn't get too caught up in having it here on earth.
And what does it mean to gather riches in heaven? It means
God will reward us with forever blessings there based on
the good things we do to bring praise to Him here on earth.

*Father God, please help me to want treasure
in heaven much more than any collection
of treasures here on earth. Amen.*

Jesus Heals

*They ran through all the country bringing people
who were sick on their beds to Jesus. Wherever He went,
they would lay the sick people in the streets in the center
of town where people gather. They begged Him that
they might touch the bottom of His coat. Everyone
who did was healed. This happened in the towns and
in the cities and in the country where He went.*

MARK 6:55–56

If you're sick or a friend or loved one is sick, pray for them. Jesus had all power back in Bible times to heal people, and He still has that power today. Sometimes He doesn't heal people here on earth, but we have to remember that forever healing is promised in heaven for all who trust in Jesus as the one and only Savior from their sins. In heaven there will be no more sickness or dying (Revelation 21:4). Above all, we should pray for everyone we know to believe in Jesus and have forever life too.

*Dear Jesus, I pray for You to heal sickness and pain
here on earth, and most of all I pray for You to heal
people's hearts forever by helping them turn to
You as the only Savior from their sins. Amen.*

Be Truly Kind, Part 1

Your kindness will reward you,
but your cruelty will destroy you.
PROVERBS 11:17 NLT

Have you ever had to deal with mean girls? It's awful. Or maybe you've messed up and acted like a mean girl yourself. If you have, you need to admit your sin, apologize, and make things right with the people you hurt—and then commit to being truly kind. God loves and forgives you!

Read these reminders from God's Word:

- "Love is kind" (1 Corinthians 13:4).

- "We should do good to everyone. For sure, we should do good to those who belong to Christ" (Galatians 6:10).

- "We know what real love is because Jesus gave up his life for us. So we also ought to give up our lives for our brothers and sisters. If someone has enough money to live well and sees a brother or sister in need but shows no compassion—how can God's love be in that person? Dear children, let's not merely say that we love each other; let us show the truth by our actions" (1 John 3:16–18 NLT).

Dear Lord, please fill me with Your true kindness. Amen.

Be Truly Kind, Part 2

We who have strong faith should help those who are weak.
We should not live to please ourselves. Each of us should
live to please his neighbor. This will help him grow in faith.
ROMANS 15:1–2

Being kind to others doesn't mean you have to be close friends with every person around you. That's not even possible. And if you tried, you'd never have time for everyone and for the good things God has planned for you. Being kind to others also never means you have to agree about everything. You can agree to disagree and still show kindness and respect. When you remember that every single person in the world (no matter who they are or what they do or what their personality is like) is created and loved by God, then He helps you be truly kind and respectful to anyone who comes into your life.

Father God, please help me remember that all people
are made in Your image and are deeply loved by You.
Help me to treat everyone kindly and respectfully. Amen.

We Can't Keep Secrets from God

The eyes of the Lord are in every place,
watching the bad and the good.

PROVERBS 15:3

Are there any secrets you're trying to keep from God? We all need to ask ourselves this question sometimes. We might think we can hide doing things we know are wrong, but it's just not true. In those times, we need to focus on the fact that God sees and knows everything everywhere. Remembering this truth can help us not to sin. God is always going to see our sin, and there will be consequences. Thankfully, God loves to forgive us, like 1 John 1:9 says: "If we tell Him our sins, He is faithful and we can depend on Him to forgive us of our sins. He will make our lives clean from all sin."

Lord God, help me to love the fact that I can't keep secrets from You! It means You are always watching me because You care about me so much and want to keep me out of trouble.

God's Good Plans

Let us put every thing out of our lives that keeps us from doing what we should. Let us keep running in the race that God has planned for us. Let us keep looking to Jesus. Our faith comes from Him and He is the One Who makes it perfect. He did not give up when He had to suffer shame and die on a cross. He knew of the joy that would be His later. Now He is sitting at the right side of God.

HEBREWS 12:1–2

What things in your life are keeping you from doing what you should? Maybe it's video games or time on your phone. Or maybe sports or activities are robbing the time you could be spending with God and loved ones and on homework and chores. God has good plans for all of us, but we have to look to Jesus and get rid of the stuff that keeps us away from those plans.

Dear Father God, I want to stay on the path You've set out for me and carry out Your special plans for my life. Please help me to get rid of anything in my life that's keeping me from them. Amen.

When You Feel All Alone

At my first trial no one helped me. Everyone left me.
I hope this will not be held against them. But the Lord was
with me. He gave me power to preach the Good News so
all the people who do not know God might hear. I was
taken from the mouth of the lion. The Lord will look after
me and will keep me from every sinful plan they have.
He will bring me safe into His holy nation of heaven.

2 TIMOTHY 4:16–18

When you feel all alone, with no one to help you, you can read and remember these words that Paul wrote in the Bible. Even though no other person was there to help, God Himself was with Paul and protected him and gave him power. Paul realized that no matter what happened on earth, someday God would bring him into heaven forever. Paul wrote this passage in his letter to Timothy to teach him about God's protection, but his words apply just as much to you today.

Lord God, I trust that no matter what happens here
in this world, You will always be with me and keep
me safe. Someday You are going to bring me into
perfect paradise in heaven with You! Amen.

Be Happy about It

If men speak bad of you because you are a Christian, you will be happy because the Spirit of shining-greatness and of God is in you. . . . But if a man suffers as a Christian, he should not be ashamed. He should thank God that he is a Christian.

1 PETER 4:14, 16

You might be mocked and teased for being a Christian, but you can be happy about it! Maybe suffering for your beliefs doesn't seem like something to be happy about, but God's Word says we should not be ashamed; we should be thankful instead! It means God's Spirit is in us and that we are saved forever. So don't worry about what anyone says or does to you. Matthew 5:11–12 (NLT) says, "God blesses you when people mock you and persecute you and lie about you and say all sorts of evil things against you because you are my followers. Be happy about it! Be very glad! For a great reward awaits you in heaven."

Dear Jesus, help me not to get angry or to feel ashamed if people tease me or act mean because I love and follow You. Remind me to be happy because You have saved me, and my reward in heaven will be great. Amen.

Truly Strong

[The Lord] answered me, "I am all you need. I give you
My loving-favor. My power works best in weak people."
I am happy to be weak and have troubles so I can have
Christ's power in me. I receive joy when I am weak.
I receive joy when people talk against me and make it
hard for me and try to hurt me and make trouble for me.
I receive joy when all these things come to me because
of Christ. For when I am weak, then I am strong.
2 Corinthians 12:9–10

God doesn't want us to be strong on our own, but it's not
because He's mean and selfish. It's because He wants us to
be truly strong, the best kind of strong—strong because we
are full of His power, not our own. He doesn't want just good
things for us; He wants the *very best* things for us—and the
best things are always found in Him!

Almighty God, help me to be happy to be weak on my
own. I'm only truly strong when I'm depending on You
for everything. Thank You for wanting the very best for
me and filling me with Your power and love. Amen.

Like Shining Gold

In a big house there are not only things made of gold and silver, but also of wood and clay. Some are of more use than others. Some are used every day. If a man lives a clean life, he will be like a dish made of gold. He will be respected and set apart for good use by the owner of the house. Turn away from the sinful things young people want to do. Go after what is right. Have a desire for faith and love and peace. Do this with those who pray to God from a clean heart.

2 TIMOTHY 2:20–22

In your quiet time today, focus on this scripture and how you want God to use your life. Do you want to be like regular everyday wood and clay, or do you want to be like shining gold used for the most amazing purposes? When you work hard to live a clean life, staying as far away from sin as possible, God can use you for the very best things He has planned.

Father God, please keep showing me any areas of my life that need to be cleaned up. Help me to stay far away from things that are bad for me. Use my life in the wonderful ways You've planned. Amen.

Your Attitude Matters

Be happy in your hope. Do not give up when trouble comes. Do not let anything stop you from praying.

ROMANS 12:12

Does anything have you feeling bummed today? If so, it's no wonder, since life involves all kinds of hard and sad things that disappoint us and get us down. We can get discouraged easily, but we can choose to be positive in the midst of the bummers. God's Word can help us. Romans 12:12 tells us that even if what's going on in our lives isn't happy, we can be happy in our hope in Jesus. We can choose never to give up, even when troubles come. And we can keep on praying, no matter what, because God never leaves us and always wants us to talk to Him and ask for His help.

Dear Jesus, please empower me to demonstrate a happy-in-hope, never-giving-up, always-praying-to-You attitude in my life. I know I can only have this kind of attitude with Your help. Amen.

Be Easygoing

*Put out of your life all these things: bad feelings
about other people, anger, temper, loud talk,
bad talk which hurts other people, and bad
feelings which hurt other people. You must
be kind to each other. Think of the other person.
Forgive other people just as God forgave you
because of Christ's death on the cross.*

EPHESIANS 4:31–32

Would you call yourself easygoing? Do you get angry easily
when plans you were looking forward to have to change?
Maybe your family had to cancel a vacation because of illness,
or there was no money for the private lessons you wanted
because of a job loss in your family. Of course you'll feel sad
or upset about those kinds of things, but you can hold on to
anger and a bad mood, or you can be easygoing, forgiving,
and understanding when your family is going through a hard
time. Anger and grumpiness will just make a bad situation
worse, but being easygoing, accepting, and loving will bless
you and everyone around you.

*Father God, when I'm sad or angry that plans
have to change, please help me choose to
have a good attitude and to show forgiveness,
understanding, and love. Amen.*

Let Yourself Cry

Then Jesus cried.
JOHN 11:35

Do you ever feel like crying but you're not sure why? Sometimes the need to cry is a result of frustration or sadness. Maybe you just need time and space to feel those emotions and give them to God in prayer. If we bottle up our emotions, they often explode in other ways or make us feel sick inside. So don't ever think that crying just means you're wimpy. Listening to your emotions, figuring out where they're coming from, and giving them time and space to release actually takes a lot of maturity and courage. When you can name your emotions and pinpoint their source, they don't have to scare you or make you act out in ways that might get you in trouble. Telling God and a trusted grown-up who cares about you all about your emotions is one of the very best ways to deal with them.

Lord God, give me wisdom and courage when it comes to the need to cry. Help me listen to my emotions and figure out how to handle them in healthy ways. Amen.

Serve Others, Serve Jesus

*"Those that are right with God will say,
'Lord, when did we see You hungry and feed You?
When did we see You thirsty and give You a drink?
When did we see You a stranger and give You a
room? When did we see You had no clothes and we
gave You clothes? And when did we see You sick or
in prison and we came to You?' Then the King will
say, 'For sure, I tell you, because you did it to one of
the least of My brothers, you have done it to Me.'"*

MATTHEW 25:37–40

Jesus taught that whenever those who love Him help someone in need, they're really helping Jesus Himself. So who in
your life is needy right now? What can you do to help and
encourage those people? If you can't think of anyone, ask
God to show you who He wants you to help and the best
ways to do so.

. . . .

***Dear Jesus, thank You that I can serve You and
show my love for You by serving others.***

Equal

You are now children of God because you have put your trust in Christ Jesus. All of you who have been baptized to show you belong to Christ have become like Christ. God does not see you as a Jew or as a Greek. He does not see you as a servant or as a person free to work. He does not see you as a man or as a woman. You are all one in Christ.

GALATIANS 3:26–28

In your quiet time today, ask God to teach you about real equality. Because of sin in the world, people will never get equality exactly right here on earth. Bad people will always try to say that some groups of people are better than others. But don't ever listen to or join them. In God's eyes, every single person is the same in value. Each one of us matters so much to God that He sent Jesus to die to save us from our sins. And when anyone trusts in Jesus, they become a child of the one true God, the King of all kings. That makes all followers of Jesus equal in royalty, and we should want to share that awesome truth with everyone we can!

Father God, You offer the only true equality through Jesus. Thank You that anyone can be Your child by trusting that only Jesus saves. Amen.

Only One Thanked Jesus

Ten men with a bad skin disease came to Him. . . .
They called to Him, "Jesus! Teacher! Take pity on us!"
When Jesus saw them, He said, "Go and show yourselves
to the religious leaders." As they went, they were healed.
One of them turned back when he saw he was healed.
He thanked God with a loud voice. He got down on
his face at the feet of Jesus and thanked Him. . . . Jesus
asked, "Were there not ten men who were healed?
Where are the other nine? Is this stranger from another
country the only one who turned back to give thanks
to God?" Then Jesus said to him, "Get up and go on
your way. Your trust in God has healed you."

LUKE 17:12–19

Ten men had been miraculously healed by Jesus. You'd think
they would have been so very excited and grateful to Him.
Yet only one of them turned back to Jesus to actually say
thank You and worship Him. In whatever ways God blesses
us, we should always want to be like the one man and not
the other nine!

. . . .

Lord God, please help me never to forget to
give You thanks for all You do for me! I am
so grateful, and every day I want to worship
and praise You for everything. Amen.

When You Feel Sad

Why are you sad, O my soul? Why have you become troubled within me? Hope in God, for I will praise Him again for His help of being near me. O my God, my soul is troubled within me. So I remember You from the land of the Jordan and the tops of Hermon, from Mount Mizar. . . . The Lord will send His loving-kindness in the day. And His song will be with me in the night, a prayer to the God of my life.

PSALM 42:5–6, 8

Sometimes we just feel sad. Life is full of hard and painful things that get us down and make us cry. We have to take that sadness to God and talk to Him about it. He'll help us remember how He has carried us through hard things in the past with His love and kindness, and we can trust that He will again and again, whenever we need Him to.

Dear Lord, when I'm sad and worried, please help me put my hope back in You, because You've shown me that You will always carry me through. Amen.

Know Your Enemy

The devil is working against you. He is walking around like a hungry lion with his mouth open. He is looking for someone to eat. Stand against him and be strong in your faith.

1 PETER 5:8–9

This scripture shares the hard truth that we Christians definitely have an enemy—the devil—who is like a hungry lion who wants to destroy us. We need to know about him and have courage to fight him. And how do we fight him? By staying close to God. Read His Word, pray continually, and be involved in a Bible-teaching church that helps you grow closer to God. Nurture good friendships with people who encourage and support you in your faith, and be very careful to keep distance from people who might lead you in bad ways. The devil wants to destroy us by getting us alone or with bad influences and tempting us to disobey God. But we can stand up to him and fight with the power God gives us!

Father God, please help me to watch out for the devil and to be ready to fight him in Your power. Amen.

A Great and Full Life

*[Jesus said,] "The robber comes only to steal and to kill and
to destroy. I came so they might have life, a great full life."*
JOHN 10:10

No matter what the devil tries to do to us, he cannot win. We
will always win against him in the end. He might hurt us or
make us stumble away from God at times, but he will never
totally defeat us when we trust in Jesus as our Savior. This
scripture tells us that the devil, who is the robber, wants to
steal and destroy every good thing, but Jesus came to give
us a great and full life. When Jesus died and then rose again,
He showed that absolutely nothing the devil does can ever
defeat the powerful love of God and His desire to give us
everlasting life with Him!

*Dear Lord, thank You so much that Jesus rose to
life again after death! He is proof of Your gift of
eternal life for me. Nothing can ever take away
that most valuable gift. Your power and love are
amazing, and I'm so grateful for them! Amen.*

God Gives So That You Can Give

God will give you enough so you can always give to others. Then many will give thanks to God for sending gifts through us. This gift you give not only helps Christians who are in need, but it also helps them give thanks to God. You are proving by this act of love what you are. They will give thanks to God for your gift to them and to others. This proves you obey the Good News of Christ. They will pray for you with great love because God has given you His loving-favor. Thank God for His great Gift.

2 CORINTHIANS 9:11–15

Every gift and blessing you receive comes from God, and He wants you to pass on those gifts and blessings. Share them with others, whether that means giving money or food to people in need, serving at church, or sharing your talents with others. Your giving shows God's love and helps more and more people come to trust in Jesus as Savior.

Dear Jesus, You are the greatest gift, and You have given me all my gifts and blessings. I want to share them with others and help them get to know You as Savior. Amen.

When You Help Your Friends

As iron sharpens iron, so a friend sharpens a friend.
PROVERBS 27:17 NLT

In your quiet time today, think of some ways you and your friends help each other. Maybe you're awesome at math but a friend gets easily confused by it, so you help her with homework. Maybe you struggle to write essays but you have a friend who is good at giving you pointers to improve. Kindness and help among friends are wonderful gifts! But they also require wisdom from God—because what if your friend asked you to do all of her math homework for her? That's no longer helping; that's actually hurting her. It's okay if she needs *some* help, but it's not okay for her to expect someone else to do her own work for her. And you should never expect that either. As you share kindness and help with your friends, always keep asking God to give you wisdom.

Father God, please help me to know when to step in to help friends and when to be a bigger help by letting them do things on their own to learn and grow. Amen.

Think Back and Remember

*Moses said to the people, "Remember this day in which
you went out of Egypt, out of the land where you
were made to stay and work. For the Lord brought
you out of this place by a powerful hand."*

EXODUS 13:3

We often just want to forget the bad things that have happened to us because they were awful and we're just so glad
they're over. But sometimes we do need to remember how
God helped us through them. Looking back and remembering strengthens our faith and helps us trust that God will be
there to rescue us again in the future. Moses told the people
of Israel to remember the awesome day that God finally
brought them out of slavery in Egypt. Just like they did, we
need to remember the amazing ways God has rescued us
from hard things too.

*Almighty God, every bit of help and rescue I have
ever received has ultimately come from You,
through so many ways and so many people!
I don't ever want to forget, and I trust You to
help and rescue me again and again! Amen.*

Don't Get Tired of Doing Good

Do not let yourselves get tired of doing good.
If we do not give up, we will get what is coming
to us at the right time. Because of this, we should
do good to everyone. For sure, we should
do good to those who belong to Christ.
GALATIANS 6:9–10

Sometimes we might feel like giving up on doing the right thing. So many people who never help others or who break the rules and do bad things seem to live good lives without getting caught or punished, and watching their example can tempt us to do the same thing or to get really discouraged. So we have to remember that God's Word tells us not to get tired of doing good. If we don't give up on following Jesus, God will bless us at exactly the right time with exactly the things He knows we need—and He will give us true, forever joy.

Dear Father God, I need Your help never to get
tired of following Your Word and Your ways.
Please encourage me and remind me that the main
reason I do good things is to make You happy
because You love me more than anyone and I want
to obey You to show my love back to You. Amen.

Look Up to Jesus Most of All

*The one who says he belongs to Christ should
live the same kind of life Christ lived.*

1 JOHN 2:6

In your quiet time today, think of your favorite famous people. Are they athletes, actors, artists, and/or musicians? What are all the things you know about them, and why are you their fan? Thinking about the lives of famous people can be so fun when we also use wisdom in looking up to celebrities. We should never become overly focused on them to the point we practically worship them. They're not perfect, and we should never forget that. Jesus is the one and only perfect famous person, and He alone should be our very favorite famous person. Only Jesus should be the one we worship and try our best to live like.

*Lord God, help me to be careful about looking up
to famous people. I want Jesus to be my first and
favorite person I look up to. I want to worship
Him alone and live my life like Him. Amen.*

Looking Up to Others

Follow my way of thinking as I follow Christ.
1 CORINTHIANS 11:1

After Jesus, the most important people to look up to are the good mentors in your life. They are people who have lived longer than you who can help you through the stages of life coming up for you, since they've already been there. Your parents can be your mentors, and sometimes a great mentor can be an older sibling or grandparent or cousin or aunt or uncle. Or you can find a mentor among older friends you know through your church or activities or community. Your mentors should definitely be people who love and follow Jesus so that they teach you more about loving and following Him too.

Father God, please bring good mentors into my life—people who love You and who will help teach and guide me to live like Jesus. Thank You! Amen.

Be a Good Young Leader

*In all things show them how to live by your life and by
right teaching. You should be wise in what you say.
Then the one who is against you will be ashamed and
will not be able to say anything bad about you.*

TITUS 2:7–8

In your quiet time today, think about the different ways you
are leading others. Someone younger is always looking up
to you. So are you being a *good* leader and setting a good
example? At school, at church, in your community, and in
your activities, ask God to help you show the younger kids in
your life that you care about them. As you build friendships
with kids younger than you, you can become a great mentor
to them and point them to Jesus as you keep following Him
and they look up to and follow you.

*Dear Lord, as I look up to and follow good and wise
leaders and mentors who love You, help me to be
a good leader and mentor to others too. Amen.*

Conquering Fear, Part 1

Show me Your loving-kindness, O God. . . .
When I am afraid, I will trust in You.
PSALM 56:1, 3

Can you think of a fear you used to have but then you got over it? How did God help you? Who were the people and what were the things God provided to get you through it? It's so good to take quiet time every once in a while to focus on things you used to be afraid of that now seem like no big deal. It helps you realize that one day soon, whatever is making you scared today will probably be no big deal. God never leaves you alone. He is right there with you in the middle of your fears, and you can call out for His help anytime. He will guide you through each hard situation to the other side, where you can look back with joy and say, "Wow! Thanks, Lord! We conquered that together, and now I'm not afraid anymore!"

Lord God, please help me with these fears I have: _____. I remember all the ways You've helped me get over fears in the past, and I'm trusting You will help me again. Amen.

Conquering Fear, Part 2

Even if I walk through the valley of the shadow of death,
I will not be afraid of anything, because You are with me.

PSALM 23:4

When you're working on conquering a fear, focus on God through His Word and prayer and praise. In your quiet time today, focus on scriptures about fear like these and repeat them, pray them, and sing them:

- "The Lord is my light and the One Who saves me. Whom should I fear? The Lord is the strength of my life. Of whom should I be afraid?" (Psalm 27:1).

- "God is our safe place and our strength. He is always our help when we are in trouble. So we will not be afraid, even if the earth is shaken and the mountains fall into the center of the sea, and even if its waters go wild with storm and the mountains shake with its action" (Psalm 46:1–3).

When your mind is focused on God, it doesn't have time to focus on fear.

Dear Father God, when I feel afraid, remind
me to keep thinking about You and Your Word,
praying to You, and praising You. Amen.

When Fear Is Good

Good thinking will keep you safe. Understanding will watch over you. You will be kept from the sinful man, and from the man who causes much trouble by what he says. You will be kept from the man who leaves the right way to walk in the ways of darkness.

PROVERBS 2:11–13

Sometimes fear can be good for you. It can keep you out of danger and trouble. You don't have to fear a backyard campfire, but you should fear fire in the way that you know you should never play around with it and start a dangerous blaze. Another example: You should fear what would happen if you were to listen to some friends who wanted to break the rules and sneak out of school. That's a good fear to listen to, because you sure don't want to get in big trouble for a dumb choice like that. God can use fear to keep you away from what would be harmful or foolish for you, so keep on asking Him to show you the times when you should listen to fear.

Dear Lord, please help me to know when fear is good for me because You're using it to keep me safe and out of trouble. Thank You for watching over me so well! Amen.

Don't Be Fake

Don't just pretend to love others. Really love them. Hate what is wrong. Hold tightly to what is good. Love each other with genuine affection, and take delight in honoring each other.

ROMANS 12:9–10 NLT

You probably know some people who seem fake. They say nice things some of the time, but they do mean things a lot of the time. They sound kind and loving, but they don't truly act kind and loving. When we deal with those people, we should learn lessons on how *not* to be. We should want to be real and sincere, honest and genuine in everything we do. Yes, we'll mess up sometimes and we'll need grace, but we should always be trying our best not to be fake. We shouldn't pretend to love others—we should truly love them with God's love.

. . . .

Father God, please forgive me for the times I've lied and been dishonest and fake with my words and actions toward others. Fill me with real love—Your love. Amen.

Awesome God

*The heavens were made by the Word of the Lord. All the
stars were made by the breath of His mouth. He gathers
the waters of the sea together as in a bag. He places the
waters in store-houses. Let all the earth fear the Lord.
Let all the people of the world honor Him. For He spoke,
and it was done. He spoke with strong words, and it stood
strong. The Lord brings the plans of nations to nothing.
He wrecks the plans of the people. The plans of the Lord
stand forever. The plans of His heart stand through the
future of all people. Happy is the nation whose God is the
Lord. Happy are the people He has chosen for His own.*
PSALM 33:6–12

Focus on God's greatness in your quiet time today, like this
psalm describes. He's more awesome than we can possibly
imagine! Nothing and no one is like almighty God. Nothing
can stop Him and His perfect plans. And all who belong to
Him are blessed forever!

. . . .

***Almighty God, You are awesome, and I'm
so blessed to be Your child. Amen.***

Slow Down When You're Angry, Part 1

If you are angry, do not let it become sin.
Get over your anger before the day is finished.

EPHESIANS 4:26

Everyone gets angry sometimes, and the Bible doesn't say anger is always bad. God knows we will and should be angry sometimes. But the Bible does say not to sin when we are angry. That can be a super hard instruction to obey! So the moment we feel anger start to rise up inside, we need to train ourselves to take big deep breaths and slow down—then pray and ask God how we should respond. His Word says in Proverbs 14:29, "He who is slow to get angry has great understanding, but he who has a quick temper makes his foolish way look right." And James 1:19 says, "Everyone should listen much and speak little. He should be slow to become angry."

Dear Lord, please remind me to slow down when
I start to feel angry. Help me to stop and ask You
how to handle it. I don't want to sin when I'm angry;
I want to deal with my anger in ways that honor
You and share Your truth and love. Amen.

Slow Down When You're Angry, Part 2

*God has chosen you. You are holy and loved by Him.
Because of this, your new life should be full of loving-
pity. You should be kind to others and have no pride.
Be gentle and be willing to wait for others. Try to
understand other people. Forgive each other. If you have
something against someone, forgive him. That is the
way the Lord forgave you. And to all these things, you
must add love. Love holds everything and everybody
together and makes all these good things perfect.*
COLOSSIANS 3:12–14

Think of some specific things that have made you angry
lately, and then think of ways you could replace the anger
with something good. What if a sibling or friend acts mean
for no reason? You could choose to be mean back, or you
could choose to be a peacemaker and suggest something
fun to do together instead of fighting. If the sibling or friend
won't stop being mean, then you can choose to walk away
or calmly get a grown-up to help. Ask God to guide you in
any kind of situation that makes you angry. He can help you
find a way to turn it into something good.

*Father God, please help me when I'm mad. I want
to make the situation better, not worse. Amen.*

Get Good Rest

On the seventh day God ended His work which He
had done. And He rested on the seventh day from
all His work which He had done. Then God honored
the seventh day and made it holy, because in it He
rested from all His work which He had done.
GENESIS 2:2–3

You might feel annoyed by bedtimes and by grown-ups trying to make sure you get enough sleep. *What's the big deal?* you might think. But getting plenty of rest really is a big deal. God thought it was such a big deal, He set aside an entire day of the week for it! You need good rest for physical and spiritual health. God wants you to have rest for actual sleep for your body and also for time spent quietly with Him, simply focusing on how great He is and how much He loves you!

Lord God, please help me to be thankful for rest
time rather than annoyed by it. You designed it,
and it's so good for me. Thank You! Amen.

Struggling in School?

*You should be happy when you have all kinds of tests.
You know these prove your faith. It helps you not to
give up. . . . If you do not have wisdom, ask God for it.*
JAMES 1:2–3, 5

Are you struggling in a certain subject in school? If not, praise and thank God for that blessing in your quiet time today. But if you are struggling in school, life can feel so stressful when you're just not "getting it." Ask God to help you continue to do your best and try your hardest while also being patient with yourself. Keep studying and practicing, and God might suddenly help you make the connections in your brain. Or He will lead you to the right grown-up or tutor or friend who knows how to explain things in just the right way for you. The most important thing is to not give up. You will get through this. You might not understand *yet*, but eventually, with God's help, you will!

- -

**Dear Father God, please help me as I try to
learn new and hard things. Help me not
to give up before I've "got it"! Amen.**

Focus on Faith Heroes

Faith shows the reality of what we hope for; it is the evidence of things we cannot see. Through their faith, the people in days of old earned a good reputation.

HEBREWS 11:1–2 NLT

In your quiet time today, think about the people among your family and friends who have super strong faith in God, those who are still living and those who have passed away. We can gain so much wisdom and encouragement by learning from them. Hebrews 11 is a wonderful passage of scripture to help us remember a whole list of great faith heroes of Bible times—people like Noah and Moses and Joseph and Sarah and Rahab, who continued to believe in God and His promises even during the worst of times in their lives. Like them, we should want to hold on to our faith no matter what. Spend time reading more about these heroes of faith, and follow their examples!

Dear Lord, please help me to remember everyone who has gone before me who kept great faith in You. I want to be strong in my faith too. Amen.

God Makes Weak Faith Stronger

"Lord, I have faith. Help my weak faith to be stronger!"
MARK 9:24

If you ever struggle to understand what God is doing or not doing about what you're praying for, it's so good to remember this story from the Bible: A father was asking Jesus for help for his son, but it was hard for the man to imagine that Jesus could do what he was asking. The father said to Jesus, "Have mercy on us and help us, if you can." Jesus replied, "What do you mean, 'If I can'? . . . Anything is possible if a person believes" (Mark 9:22–23 NLT). And the father said, "Lord, I have faith. Help my weak faith to be stronger!" When we pray, we have to remember that God is able to do exactly what we ask and so much more! He may or may not answer the way we hope, but no matter how He responds to our prayers, our main response to God should be, "Lord, I have faith. Help my weak faith to be stronger!"

Lord God, please make my faith stronger and stronger each day. I believe anything is possible with You! Amen.

God's Guiding Word

*How sweet is Your Word to my taste! It is sweeter than honey
to my mouth! I get understanding from Your Law and so I
hate every false way. Your Word is a lamp to my feet and a
light to my path. I have promised that I will keep Your Law.
And I will add strength to this promise. . . . My life is always
in my hand, yet I do not forget Your Law. The sinful have set
a trap for me, yet I have not turned from Your Law. I have
been given Your Law forever. It is the joy of my heart. I have
set my heart on obeying Your Law forever, even to the end.*
PSALM 119:103–106, 109–112

Is God's Word what is really, truly lighting your path and
leading the way in your life? God wants us all to love His
Word and find joy in following it. The Bible is our guidebook
for the best kind of life, with blessings and rewards both
now and forever.

*Father God, help me to love Your Word and
follow it more closely each day of my life as
I grow in relationship with You! Amen.*

Joy in the Hard Times

*With this hope you can be happy even if you need to
have sorrow and all kinds of tests for awhile. These tests
have come to prove your faith and to show that it is good.
Gold, which can be destroyed, is tested by fire. Your faith
is worth much more than gold and it must be tested also.
Then your faith will bring thanks and shining-greatness and
honor to Jesus Christ when He comes again. You have never
seen Him but you love Him. You cannot see Him now but you
are putting your trust in Him. And you have joy so great
that words cannot tell about it. You will get what your faith is
looking for, which is to be saved from the punishment of sin.*

1 PETER 1:6–9

Even in the midst of hard times, we can have happiness and
joy. Hard times are tests that show whether our faith in Jesus
is real or fake. It's easy to say we love and trust Jesus when
we have no problems, but keeping faith during hard times
shows that we *truly* trust in Him.

*Dear Jesus, even when life is hard, and even though
I don't see You in person, I will keep on trusting
You. My faith in You is real, not fake. Amen.*

Tough Times with Tough Leaders

*Open your heart to teaching, and your
ears to words of much learning.*

PROVERBS 23:12

Throughout your years of growing up, you're going to have
some teachers and coaches who are wonderful to learn
from—and some who definitely aren't. Maybe right now
you can think of a particular teacher or coach who is just so
hard to learn from. Maybe their rules and assignments and
expectations all seem like too much. But if they're just strict,
you might learn a whole lot if you just keep showing respect.
God cares about your situation. Ask Him to help things get
better—whether that means the teacher or coach changes
their ways or you simply do your best to adapt. Let God show
you how to communicate well with your teacher or coach
as you make the most of a tough situation.

*Dear Father God, please help me make it through
this tough time with a difficult leader. Help me to do
my best and show respect, even when I don't feel like
it. Please help the situation to improve, and make me
stronger and wiser as a result of this experience. Amen.*

Get Organized

We always pray and give thanks to God for you.
COLOSSIANS 1:3

If you like to be super organized (or just need to get better at it), you can organize prayer topics for your quiet time. With either art supplies or a computer program, design a calendar. Once you have it ready, fill it up with specific names of people to pray for and topics and concerns in the world: family members, friends, neighbors, teachers, instructors, coaches, pastors and church leaders and volunteers, police and military, missionaries, health care providers—the list goes on and on! You might be surprised by how quickly you fill it up. And of course you can list names and topics more than once. The point is, find creative ways to remember to pray for the specific people and concerns in your life. You can never pray too much!

Dear Lord, help me to get organized and remember specific people and requests in prayer. Thank You for caring about everyone and about everything going on in our world and in our lives. Amen.

God Never Gets Tired

*The God Who lives forever is the Lord, the One Who made
the ends of the earth. He will not become weak or tired.
His understanding is too great for us to begin to know.
He gives strength to the weak. And He gives power to him
who has little strength. Even very young men get tired
and become weak and strong young men trip and fall.
But they who wait upon the Lord will get new strength.
They will rise up with wings like eagles. They will run and
not get tired. They will walk and not become weak.*

ISAIAH 40:28–31

No matter how much energy we wake up with every day, it
always runs out. Whether we like it or not, we have to sleep.
Only God never gets tired. He's amazing! Yes, we need physical
rest, but also we need to come to Him in quiet time so that
He can give us spiritual rest and a fresh jolt of spiritual energy!

*Almighty God, I praise You for Your awesome, endless
power, Your energy that never runs out! Please give me
new spiritual strength and energy each day. Amen.*

Don't Be a Show-Off

"When you pray, do not be as those who pretend to be someone they are not. They love to stand and pray in the places of worship or in the streets so people can see them. . . . When you pray, go into a room by yourself. After you have shut the door, pray to your Father Who is in secret. Then your Father Who sees in secret will reward you."

MATTHEW 6:5–6

You've probably encountered show-offs in your life—people who try to keep all the attention on themselves. Jesus talked about the kinds of people who even use prayer to show off. And He said not to be like them. Our prayers and quiet time should be a sincere conversation with our heavenly Father, a time of praising Him and asking for His help and learning from Him.

Does this scripture passage mean that every single prayer should be said in secret, when we're alone? No, but it is making the point that prayer should be sincere and only to our one true God. And in every prayer we should want all attention on God and His power alone, not on ourselves.

Lord God, help me to put all attention on You in prayer and praise! Amen.

Be Faithful Like Daniel

*He got down on his knees three times
each day, praying and giving thanks
to his God, as he had done before.*

DANIEL 6:10

Daniel in the Bible is an awesome example of faithfulness in
quiet time. Three times each day he prayed and gave thanks
to God. Even when he knew he might be thrown into a den of
lions for praying, he never stopped. And then he *was* thrown
into that den. But God shut the mouths of the lions so they
didn't harm Daniel—amazing! And even more, the next day
King Darius was so astonished by this miracle that he chose
to believe in God and announced that all the people of his
nation should too!

*Dear Father God, help me to be brave and devoted
like Daniel, who never stopped praying to You even
when he was in great danger for being faithful to
You. Please also let me see great miracles happen
when I follow You no matter what! Amen.*

Friends Near and Far

Two people are better off than one, for they can help each
other succeed. If one person falls, the other can reach out
and help. But someone who falls alone is in real trouble.
ECCLESIASTES 4:9–10 NLT

It's such a bummer when good friends move away. Has that happened to you? Thankfully, these days it's much easier to keep in touch with friends even after a move, but still, friendship does change when you live far apart. Or maybe a friend has changed or rejected you and you're not friends anymore. That's so hard and sad. To lose closeness with a friend might cause you to feel scared to reach out and make more friends, but don't give in to that fear. Ask God to help bring a new good friend or two into your life. He will answer and provide who you need when you wait patiently on Him! He knows friendship and encouragement are important.

Lord God, please comfort me when I'm sad and
missing a friend who has moved away or mourning
a friendship that has been broken. Please bring
me new friends to enjoy life with. Amen.

Highs and Lows

Is anyone among you suffering? He should pray.
Is anyone happy? He should sing songs of thanks to God.
JAMES 5:13

If you're ever stuck and not sure what to say to God during your quiet time with Him, try playing a little game of High Low. Tell Him the high or best part of your day. And then tell Him the low or worst part. Even though He was with you through it all, He loves for you to talk to Him about anything and everything. Invite God into your thoughts and feelings, knowing that He's already constantly present with you anyway and loves to be welcomed by you. When you're sharing about the different events of the day and how they made you feel, give any worries or fears or needs to God and praise Him for all the good things. He cares about every high and every low and everything in between.

Father God, please help me to remember Your constant presence with me. I welcome You into every part of my life. I love You and need You so much! Amen.

God Will Never Leave You

God has said, "I will never leave you or let you be alone." So we can say for sure, "The Lord is my Helper. I am not afraid of anything man can do to me."

HEBREWS 13:5–6

People we love often say to us (and we say this to those we love too), "I'm always here for you." It's an awesome show of love and loyalty and support. But sometimes, even though we try our hardest, it's just not possible to *always* be there for others because we are human and not capable of being perfect. Only God can make that promise to absolutely never ever leave us. And He will never go back on that promise, not even accidentally. Even if you don't feel Him with you at times, He is. Just keep calling out to Him in prayer and listening for Him, especially through His Word.

Where would I be without You as my Helper, Lord? I can't thank You enough for never leaving me alone. Remind me that I never need to be afraid of anything, because You are always with me, always helping me, always protecting me.

Like a Lion

*The sinful run away when no one is trying to
catch them, but those who are right with God
have as much strength of heart as a lion.*

PROVERBS 28:1

This scripture is comparing people who don't trust Jesus as Savior with people who do. If you are right with God, meaning you have asked Jesus to be your Savior, this scripture tells you that you are as bold and brave as a lion! How cool is that? And people who don't trust Jesus as Savior are often so afraid of any little thing that they're running even when there is no danger. They might not ever admit it, but deep down they have no faith to give them courage. But everyone who trusts Jesus as Savior does have faith. They are right with God because of Jesus, and so they are able to be as strong as the mightiest lion.

*Dear Jesus, I trust You, and I know You make me
right with God. I have nothing to fear. My heart
is brave and strong because of You! Amen.*

God Cares about Your Sorrows

*You keep track of all my sorrows. You have
collected all my tears in your bottle.
You have recorded each one in your book.*
PSALM 56:8 NLT

Through every hard and sad thing in life that makes us cry,
we must believe that God cares about each of our sorrows.
The Bible promises He is near when we are brokenhearted,
and He heals us (Psalm 34:18; 147:3). He knows and cares
about every single one of our sad tears (Psalm 56:8). And
for all who believe in Jesus, He is preparing heaven, where
"He will wipe every tear from their eyes, and there will be no
more death or sorrow or crying or pain. All these things are
gone forever" (Revelation 21:4 NLT).

When you're hurting, pray to God and cry to Him. Let Him
collect your tears, and focus on the truth of these scriptures.
He will help you keep going and keep finding joy, and one
day He will make everything right.

*Lord God, I'm hurting and need Your comfort, and I need
to remember the truth of Your Word. Thank You for
keeping track of and caring about every tear I cry. Amen.*

Use Your Special Gifts

We all have different gifts that God has given to us by His loving-favor. We are to use them. If someone has the gift of preaching the Good News, he should preach. . . . If someone has the gift of helping others, then he should help. If someone has the gift of teaching, he should teach. If someone has the gift of speaking words of comfort and help, he should speak. If someone has the gift of sharing what he has, he should give from a willing heart. If someone has the gift of leading other people, he should lead them. If someone has the gift of showing kindness to others, he should be happy as he does it.

ROMANS 12:6–8

God has given you special gifts and talents that He wants you to use to help spread His love and bring Him praise! Maybe you've already figured out what some of those gifts are, and you might discover more as you keep growing up. Pray for God to help you be sure of the gifts He has given you, and ask Him to show you how to share them well!

Father God, help me to recognize the special gifts You've created me with. Show me how You want me to use them. Help me point many people to knowing and loving You! Amen.

173

How Long, Lord?

I wait for the Lord. My soul waits and I hope in His Word.

PSALM 130:5

Sometimes it's *so hard* to wait on God's answers to prayer. The prophet Habakkuk in the Bible felt impatient too. He prayed, "O Lord, how long must I call for help before You will hear? I cry out to You, 'We are being hurt!' But You do not save us. Why do you make me see sins and wrong-doing? People are being destroyed in anger in front of me. There is arguing and fighting. The Law is not followed. What is right is never done. For the sinful are all around those who are right and good, so what is right looks like sin" (Habakkuk 1:2–4).

We can learn from God's response that our human minds can't fully understand what God is doing while we wait for Him to answer prayer. He said to Habakkuk, "Look among the nations, and see! Be surprised and full of wonder! For I am doing something in your days that you would not believe if you were told" (Habakkuk 1:5).

*Lord God, help me to remember that You do things
my mind can never fully understand. You are
working out Your plans in exactly the right ways.
I choose to trust You no matter what. Amen.*

Real Hope and Joy

The hope of those who are right with God is joy, but the hope of the sinful comes to nothing. The way of the Lord is a strong-place to those who are faithful, but it destroys those who do wrong. Those who are right with God will never be shaken, but the sinful will not live in the land.

PROVERBS 10:28–30

Some people constantly turn away from Jesus and reject Him, yet they seem to have lives full of fun and happiness. That can be hard to watch, especially when we go through hard times that make us wonder if we should turn away from Jesus too. So we have to remember that real, lasting joy comes only from Jesus, and people who reject Him have futures that are hopeless. That's really sad. We should keep trying to point people to Jesus anyway while keeping our own faith in Him strong, no matter what, trusting Him to protect and bless us in the best ways both now and forever.

Dear Lord, help me to keep looking to You, not at those who turn away from You and reject You. I trust You, and I know that You will never stop loving me and blessing me. Amen.

A Good Name

A good name is to be chosen instead of many riches.
PROVERBS 22:1

In your quiet time today, focus on having a good name. A good name means a good reputation and good character. When people hear your name, do you want them to think of you in good ways or bad ways? Do you want to be known for things like laziness or lying or rudeness or getting into trouble? Or do you want to be known for living for Jesus, doing your best, and being kind, loving, fair, honest, and worthy of respect? Choose now while you are young to do your very best to have a good name your whole life. It doesn't mean you will always be perfect, but it means you will obey God's ways of love and fairness and honesty—and will quickly want to make things right when you make a mistake and do wrong.

Dear Father God, I want to be known for good character and a good name because I obey You. I want to have a good name and inspire people to praise Your name above all! Amen.

Everyone Knows about God

Men know about God. He has made it plain to
them. Men cannot say they do not know about God.
From the beginning of the world, men could see what
God is like through the things He has made. This shows
His power that lasts forever. It shows that He is God.
ROMANS 1:19–20

Do you know that every person knows about God simply by looking around at His creation? God has shown Himself through everything He has made in His creation. Anyone can know that God is real by simply observing all the cool details of animals and plants and mountains and forests and seas. Anyone can see Him in the incredible way our human bodies are designed and in the way animals know how to hunt for their food or build themselves a home. Our Creator God is awesome, and He deserves all of our worship and praise!

Almighty God, I love seeing Your work in all the things
You have made. Thank You for making Yourself known
through Your amazing creation! I pray that more and
more people would come to know Jesus as Savior. Amen.

You Can Be a Mighty Hero

*The angel of the LORD appeared to [Gideon] and
said, "Mighty hero, the LORD is with you!"*

JUDGES 6:12 NLT

How would you feel if someone you really looked up to gave
you a wonderful compliment? Pretty awesome, right? So
imagine how Gideon in the Bible must have felt when God
spoke to him through an angel's appearance and called him
a "mighty hero." Wow!

You can think of God telling you the same thing He told
Gideon. You are totally capable of being a mighty hero for
God. He is with you, always giving you courage and power.
Those qualities don't come from yourself but from God's
Holy Spirit in you.

*Lord God, I trust that You are with me in
everything I do. I want to be a mighty hero who
points people to You and Your love! Amen.*

Keep It Up

"If he keeps on asking, he will get up and give him as much as he needs. I say to you, ask, and what you ask for will be given to you. Look, and what you are looking for you will find. Knock, and the door you are knocking on will be opened to you. For everyone who asks, will receive what he asks for. Everyone who looks, will find what he is looking for. Everyone who knocks, will have the door opened to him."

LUKE 11:8–10

Do you wonder if God ever gets tired of you coming to Him in your quiet time and asking for things in prayer? Jesus Himself taught in the Bible that God absolutely does not! Do your parents ever get tired of you asking for things? Of course they do! No human parent could say they never get annoyed sometimes by their children's repeated requests. But God is your all-powerful, never-tiring heavenly Father, and in Luke 11, Jesus tells you to keep on asking!

Dear Father God, thank You that You never get tired of listening to my prayers and spending time with me! Amen.

Keep Growing in Good Things

*Do your best to add holy living to your faith. Then add
to this a better understanding. As you have a better
understanding, be able to say no when you need to. Do not
give up. And as you wait and do not give up, live God-like.
As you live God-like, be kind to Christian brothers and love
them. If you have all these things and keep growing in them,
they will keep you from being of no use and from having
no fruit when it comes to knowing our Lord Jesus Christ.*

2 PETER 1:5–8

You might be really social and outgoing, or you might be on
the quieter side. Both are wonderful! What matters is that
you're aware of how God made you to be and that you ask
Him to help you use the personality and gifts He's given you to
serve Him in the ways He asks. And He can grow and develop
you with new traits and gifts and skills according to His will, so
let Him! But to make the most of your gifts, you need to stay
in constant good relationship and communication with Him.
So never stop praying. Never stop reading God's Word. Never
stop learning from and serving your loving heavenly Father!

*Dear Lord, please help me to learn more about
myself and the way You designed me as I keep
learning from You and staying close to You. Amen.*

Looking in a Broken Mirror

Now that which we see is as if we were looking in a broken mirror. But then we will see everything. Now I know only a part. But then I will know everything in a perfect way. That is how God knows me right now.

1 CORINTHIANS 13:12

When you're praying in your quiet time and asking God for answers but not understanding His ways, this verse is so important to remember. Everything in this world is broken from the perfect way God intended it, because sin entered the world when Adam and Eve chose to disobey God. And the way that we see and try to understand is broken because of sin too. But God is working out His plans, and at just the right time He will make all things new and right. Then we will see things perfectly as He does, and the view will be amazing!

Lord God, help me to trust You even when I'm confused and hurting. Please give me peace that at just the right time, You will make everything right and good forever. Amen.

Be Still and Know

God is our refuge and strength, always ready to help in times of trouble. So we will not fear when earthquakes come and the mountains crumble into the sea. Let the oceans roar and foam. Let the mountains tremble as the waters surge!... God's voice thunders, and the earth melts! The Lord of Heaven's Armies is here among us; the God of Israel is our fortress. Come, see the glorious works of the Lord.... "Be still, and know that I am God! I will be honored by every nation. I will be honored throughout the world." The Lord of Heaven's Armies is here among us; the God of Israel is our fortress.
PSALM 46:1–3, 6–8, 10–11 NLT

How often do you stop to think about God's awesome greatness and power? Right now, be still and think about how nothing is mightier than God is. Nothing is ever out of His control, and He cares about every big and tiny detail of your life. He is your strength and safe place no matter where you are or what you're going through.

Father God, I just want to sit and think about how awesome You are today. I praise You, and I'm so grateful for You! Amen.

Should We Keep On Sinning?

Well then, should we keep on sinning so that God can show us more and more of his wonderful grace? Of course not!
ROMANS 6:1–2 NLT

When we ask God for forgiveness for the wrong things we've done, He forgives us fully and reassures us of His love. Because of God's great kindness, we might think it's no big deal to keep sinning and then just ask for more forgiveness. But if we truly love God, we'll want to obey Him and honor Him, not choose bad things again and again with a "who cares?" attitude. We are definitely going to mess up and make bad choices sometimes, but we should feel sad about sin and the way it hurts God. Then we should do our best not to sin in the future. Also, even though God always forgives when we ask, He doesn't always keep us from the consequences of bad choices. Ask God to help you keep running away from sin; don't play around with it like it doesn't matter.

Lord God, I know You love me no matter what, but I don't want to sin against You on purpose and pretend it's no big deal. Please help me to keep growing in my understanding of Your wonderful grace. Amen.

What God Gives to Fight With

*Be strong with the Lord's strength. . . . Our fight. . .
is against the demon world that works in the heavens.
Because of this, put on all the things God gives you to
fight with. Then you will be able to stand in that sinful
day. When it is all over, you will still be standing. So stand
up and do not be moved. Wear a belt of truth around
your body. Wear a piece of iron over your chest which
is being right with God. Wear shoes on your feet which
are the Good News of peace. Most important of all, you
need a covering of faith in front of you. This is to put out
the fire-arrows of the devil. The covering for your head
is that you have been saved from the punishment of sin.
Take the sword of the Spirit which is the Word of God.*

Ephesians 6:10, 12–17

These verses can sound scary, but we don't need to be
scared of anything when we have God's protection. Focus
on this passage of scripture and ask God to teach you more
about what it means to wear the armor of God every day.

*Dear Lord, I want to wear all the armor, all the
spiritual protective gear that Your Word talks
about. Help me learn to trust You more and
more for strength and protection. Amen.*

Once and for All Time

Christ is not like other religious leaders. They had to give gifts every day on the altar in worship for their own sins first and then for the sins of the people. Christ did not have to do that. He gave one gift on the altar and that gift was Himself. It was done once and it was for all time.

HEBREWS 7:27

You might hear people say that all religions are the same, but it's just not true. Jesus was the only human being to live on earth who was holy and without any sin. He gave His own life to die once for all people of all time to save them from their sin. Then He rose again to show His power over death and to offer forever life to all who trust in Him. No other religion offers that kind of gift and love and miracle! To know Jesus as Savior is simply to believe in Him and accept the awesome gift of His grace, recognizing He took our sins away when He died on the cross and then rose to life again.

Dear Jesus, thank You for giving Your life to save everyone who believes in You! No one else is like You! You are God, and You are the one and only living Savior! Amen.

Don't Ever, Ever, Ever Give Up!

I did not give up waiting for the Lord. And He turned to me and heard my cry. He brought me up out of the hole of danger, out of the mud and clay. He set my feet on a rock, making my feet sure. He put a new song in my mouth, a song of praise to our God. Many will see and fear and will put their trust in the Lord. How happy is the man who has made the Lord his trust, and has not turned to the proud or to the followers of lies. O Lord my God, many are the great works You have done, and Your thoughts toward us. No one can compare with You!
Psalm 40:1–5

When we don't give up on trusting in God, even when times are hard, He will come through for us. He will rescue us from trouble. He will give us new joy and encouragement. And on top of that, He will let others see our faith in Him so that they can come to love and follow God too!

Dear God, I never want to give up on You, because You love me and never give up on me. Amen.

Scripture Index

Check Out This Fun Faith Map!

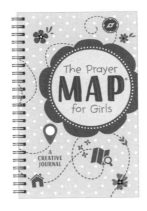

This prayer journal is a fun and creative way to fully experience the power of prayer. Each page guides you to write out thoughts, ideas, and lists. . .creating a specific "map" for you to follow as you talk to God. Each map includes a spot to record the date, so you can look back on your prayers and see how God has worked in your life.

Spiral Bound / 978-1-68322-559-1